76

THE LYNMOUTH FLOOD DISASTER

By

ERIC R. DELDERFIELD

In collaboration with
R. B. CARNEGIE, O.B.E., C.B.E.

Published by E.R.D. Publications Ltd., Exmouth.

THE LYNMOUTH FLOOD DISASTER

First Published	—	May, 1953
Second Edition	—	October, 1956
Third Edition	—	March, 1958
Fourth Edition	—	March, 1965
Fifth Edition	—	January, 1969
Sixth Edition	—	June, 1972
Seventh Edition	—	April, 1974
Eighth Edition	—	January, 1976

Printed by
John G. Eccles, Inverness, Scotland.

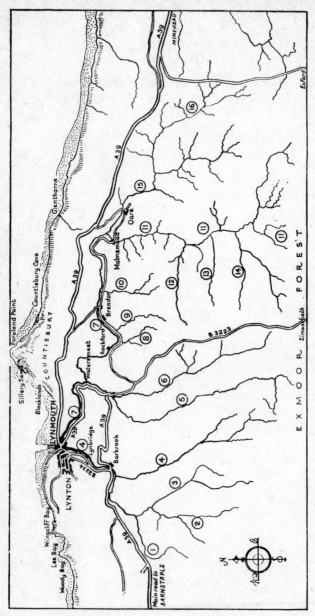

Sketch of Tributaries of the West and East Lyn Rivers

1. RANSCOMBE WATER
2. WOOLHANGER WATER
3. THORNWORTHY WATER
4. WEST LYN RIVER
5. HOAROAK WATER
6. FARLEY WATER
7. EAST LYN RIVER
8. CRANSCOMBE WATER
9. TIPPACOTT WATER
10. COOMBE LAWN WATER
11. BADGWORTHY WATER
12. LANK COOMBE WATER
13. HOCCOMBE COMBE WATER
14. HOCCOMBE WATER
15. OARE WATER
16. WEIR WATER

Copyright: E.R.D. Publications Ltd.

ILLUSTRATIONS

The name which appears in parenthesis after each picture is a grateful acknowledgement to those who have loaned pictures and allowed reproduction

PREFACE

The story of the LYNMOUTH FLOOD DISASTER had to be written, for it was an unparalleled tragedy on a great scale. When the story was well under way, the East Coast floods with their appalling loss of life occurred, but except for the fact that both were terrible disasters, the two had little in common. The Lynmouth floods were caused by rainfall and rivers, and the peculiar geographical position of the village. It was the biggest flood in the smallest area ever known in this country. The destruction and loss of life were confined in the main to a limited region, whereas on the East Coast the floods were caused by the encroaching of the sea, and covered a very wide area. Over all, however, the world-wide sentimental attachment in which Lynton and Lynmouth are held was obvious if only by the amazingly generous response to the Appeal Fund. It was necessary to set down quickly the happenings and aftermath of the night of Friday, August 15th, 1952, for already many details are forgotten.

There have been many problems, not the least the question of names of those who took part. It was impracticable to mention everyone and equally impossible to mention none. Therefore, the middle course—always dangerous—has been adopted. There is no doubt, however, that everyone present that night showed a very high standard of courage. There were many heroes and heroines who did what came to hand, and then went off unsung to assist elsewhere.

The spirit shown during and after the disaster was in accordance with the highest traditions of the British race. The comradeship and co-operation between the organisations whose members came from far and wide, was typical of that which seems to blossom only in times of war or dire trouble.

This then is the story of the Lynmouth Flood Disaster, written with no attempt at sensationalism, but straightforwardly from facts and interviews as I have gathered them, so that future generations will know what really happened and thus be able to honour those who were present and took part.

I am indeed grateful for all the assistance and willing help received in gathering the necessary data, and particularly to Mr. R. B. Carnegie who collaborated with me.

E.R.D.

April, 1953.

PREFACE TO THE EIGHTH EDITION

First published in 1953, the demand for this book has been continuous. The first edition was reprinted four times, the second third and fourth editions three times each. Now comes the eighth edition.

The Flood, of course, has become history which undoubtedly accounts for the demand of this, the only popular account of the tragedy ever written.

Over twenty years have passed since the book was written and inevitably some of the items date the story. Nevertheless, there is nothing to add to the general picture and I am content therefore merely to bring the postscript up to date.

E.R.D.

Exmouth, 1975.

CONTENTS

THE
LYNMOUTH FLOOD DISASTER

PROLOGUE

The night of Friday, August 15th, 1952, will ever be remembered in North Devon, for within a matter of hours one of the most charming and romantic villages in Britain was visited by a major calamity which became world news.

The two gentle streams which have given Lynmouth much of its character, were indirectly the cause of it all—the streams and nature in its most awful, ferocious and uncontrollable mood. High up on the hills and Exmoor Forest it had rained incessantly for hours, causing the streams to become torrents. Ninety million tons of water, sufficient to supply the needs of the immediate area for over a hundred years, cascaded down on to the village, sweeping all before it.

In one terrible night at the height of the summer season, twelve hundred residents and visitors faced death. The homes and belongings of many of them were swept away and in the darkness that ensued deeds of bravery and heroism, which one associates with the dark days of war rather than of peace, took place.

Death in its most sudden form visited the people of North Devon and Somerset that night. Damage in other areas was severe but scattered. In Lynmouth, it was concentrated on a village known for its beauty all over the world. Thousands who knew Lynmouth well, gazed with awe at the pictures of the disaster, and found themselves unable to identify familiar surroundings. The onslaught of the floods and the resulting devastation, made it impossible to get full news of the tragedy to the outside world until the next morning. Furthermore, the unique position of the village, surrounded by hills and with but two main roads approaching it, made rescue work both precarious and difficult.

When the full story was told the country was shocked, and the world's demonstrations of sympathy and practical help swamped the area, as had the floods but twenty-four hours before.

THE GROWTH OF LYNMOUTH

During the early years of the nineteenth century, when the Napoleonic Wars made visits to the continent impossible, those people who had been in the habit of going abroad for their holidays were obliged to seek alternative resorts in their own country. Someone "discovered" Lynmouth, and the beauty of this little fishing village cast an irresistible spell on those who, undaunted by its remote situation and the lack of organised transport, began to come in increasing numbers from all over England. Poets—notably Shelley (who resided there in 1812) and Southey—felt its magic charm and were inspired to write songs in praise of this lovely spot on the north coast of Devon, where nature's simplicity offered a refreshing contrast to the sophistication of the more fashionable watering-places.

The description given by Southey cannot indeed be bettered:—

> "*Two rivers join at Lynmouth. Each of these flows down a combe rolling over huge stones like a long waterfall; immediately at their junctions they enter the sea; and the river and the sea make one sound of uproar. Of these combes, the one is richly wooded, the other runs between two high, bare strong hills. From the hill between the two is a prospect most magnificent; on either hand combes; and the river before the little village . . . . . This alone would constitute a view beautiful enough to repay the weariness of a long journey; but to complete it there is the blue and boundless sea.*"

In 1869, when R. D. Blackmore wrote *Lorna Doone*, the spotlight was again thrown on the area and as time went on the

general atmosphere of romance which surrounded Lynmouth
appealed in a special way to bridal couples, so that the village
became known affectionately as the "Honeymooners' paradise".

The ever increasing number of visitors opened up a new
source of income for the residents, and instead of having to
depend primarily on the fishing which had for centuries been
the chief form of livelihood, they found that the tourist trade was
theirs for the developing.

Coaches began to ply between Lynmouth and the neigh-
bouring towns of Barnstaple and Minehead, thus affording
connections with the established routes to various parts of the
country. The fact that passengers had to get out and walk when-
ever they came to steep hills (and this was often, as those familiar
with the district today will confirm) did not deter the travellers,
but only added to the novelty of their adventure. Countisbury
Hill was then, as it is now, one of the stiffest climbs in the district, and in the coaching days of the 1850's it took six horses to
haul the vehicle to the summit. Business flourished, and the
coach proprietors served the public well. There were three
return services to Barnstaple each day, and it was very, very rare
even in the hardest weather for the three-horse bus or mail cart
to fail to complete the journey, even if the coaches were unable
to do so. They were grand and picturesque days, in which the
foundations of the modern Lynmouth were laid.

It was only to be expected, however, that rivals should
enter a field which promised such lucrative returns. Towards
the end of the century, a miniature railway was opened between
Lynton (Lynmouth's twin village) and Barnstaple so that the
journey could be undertaken in comparative comfort by those
who were unable to face the rigours of the coach trip. The railway was sponsored by Sir George Newnes, the famous publisher,
and Sir Thomas Hewitt, K.C. These two were instrumental in
forming a local company. The railway was a two foot gauge and
was officially opened on May 11th, 1898. Far exceeding the

optimistic estimates, it cost nearly £100,000 to construct and never repaid the shareholders more than one-half per cent on the capital invested.

In 1923, the concern was acquired by the London & South Western Railway Company, which—it subsequently transpired —continued to run at an increasing loss until 1935, when the Southern Railway closed it down. Once again contact between the village and the outside world was by coaches—but this time motor-coaches.

Sir George Newnes, who had long been captivated by the beauty of the district and proved a great benefactor to Lynton and Lynmouth, built a residence on Hollerday Hill in 1892. He gave the very fine Town Hall at Lynton, provided the financial backing for the building of the Cliff Railway and was active in a scheme for the building of a new harbour at Lynmouth, which unfortunately never came to fruition.

One of the greatest drawbacks in the full development of the villages was the difficulty of access between the top and bottom of the five hundred foot cliff, and the building of the Cliff railway (the first of its kind in England) in 1890 did much to improve the facilities. The railway, which is nine hundred feet long with a gradient of one in one-and-three-quarters, is a very popular and useful mode of travel with all visitors, and it is not surprising that each season the "lift" carries an average of 350,000 passengers.

As early as 1890, Lynton and Lynmouth were lit by electricity, which was generated by the largest installation driven by water power in England.

With all these improvements taking place, the fame of the villages spread more rapidly than ever and visitors from overseas began to include them in their itinerary, whilst travellers from all parts of the British Isles considered a tour of Devon or Somerset quite incomplete without a call at Lynton and Lynmouth.

Despite its popularity, however, and the unavoidable impact of new ideas and customs, Lynmouth remained comparatively unspoiled. Some of the old thatched cottages gave place, it is true, to hotels and restaurants, but the new buildings blended harmoniously with the old and soon became part of the picture. Nothing could change the salient feature of the landscape—those precipitous hills which encircle the village so closely that the dwellings had perforce to be built on the slopes, where they appear to cling perilously at varying levels. Trees are everywhere, robing the rocky heights with verdure and changing their dress in time with the seasons—dark and forbidding under wintry skies, majestic with the red and gold of autumn. But in spring and summer, when the foliage is fresh and green and the two streams, the East Lyn and the West Lyn, chatter gently as they flow swiftly but harmlessly over their stony beds encompassing, in a rough triangle, the village of Lynmouth, it is a place of enchantment, a fairy-tale country come to life.

The miniature harbour gave anchorage to a tiny fleet of fishing and sailing boats, and a picturesque touch was added by the little tower on the harbour wall, which was originally erected to guide the fishermen home. It was enlarged about a hundred years ago by General Rawden to provide storage for salt water for baths, and was increased in height and finished like the towers common on the Rhine, so that it became known as the Rhenish Tower.

The name Lynmouth is said to be derived from the Anglo-Saxon LLYNNA—a torrent, thus "Lynmouth—the town on the torrent."

Picturesque, welcoming, safe—this was the Lynmouth which captivated the hearts of all comers, so that they returned again and yet again.

In winter, the population of Lynmouth has always remained at about four hundred and fifty, but in the height of an average season the figure rises to about twelve hundred. That was the number of people resident there on the night of Friday, August 15th, 1952 when through abnormal rainfall, history of two hundred years before was repeated and the village was the centre of a disaster which created world-wide interest.

The first news of the happening was broadcast over the wireless at 7 o'clock on the morning of Saturday, August 16th, but the announcement was made in order to stop intending holiday-makers trying to get through. It was not until later in the day that the extent of the calamity and the subsequent death-roll was given to the world.

HOW IT ALL BEGAN

Much of the beauty of Exmoor and North Devon generally is provided by the lovely little streams which meander in and about the heather strewn hillsides and moorland. The stone bridges which carry the motoring roads seem small, but to the visitor who sees them in the summer, they dwarf the tiny trickle which inevitably runs beneath them.

These streams in their dozens drain the high moorland of Exmoor Forest and feed the largest rivers—rivers in name but in size no more than streams themselves. Most of these watercourses rise less then ten miles from the coast and as they trickle towards Lynmouth, which forms their outlet to the sea and the Bristol Channel, they fall some fifteen hundred feet. A glance at the sketch map on page 6 illustrates this network well. South of Lynmouth there are the rivers of Bray and Heddon, and higher up the moorland and to the east are the streams, Oare Water, Badgworthy Water and Weir Water which drain the Doone Valley. They all flow into and form the East Lyn river. In the same way, dozens of minor tributaries flow into and form the West Lyn. Both rivers converge at Lynmouth and join in the last gush to the little harbour and the sea.

North Devon's annual rainfall is well above the average of Devon and Somerset and in August 1952, that average was well maintained. High up on the thirty-nine square miles of Exmoor Forest, rain during an unusually wet month had been soaking through the heather covered peat crust and filling to overflowing the enormous sponge-like natural reservoirs. It was a process that happened periodically but even a short spell, or perhaps just a cessation of rain for a day or so, would have given respite. There was no such easing of the downpour on Friday, August 15th. It rained heavily all day and as evening drew on and darkness fell, the downpour increased in its intensity. The streams and rivers were already turbulent and swollen. By late evening it was obvious to those living on the moorlands that there was trouble afoot. About 8.30 p.m. there occurred one of those catastrophies of nature—a cloudburst. In this country an inch of rain in a short period of time is unusual, but on this occasion it was calculated that the intensity was equal to five inches in one single hour, and subsequently over nine inches were measured in the twenty-four hours. Nine inches! More than three months' normal fall.

Rivulets that in summer were a mere trickle became broad streams, small streams became large ones and the rivers themselves became raging torrents. At first, the streams and waterways overflowed their normal channels and spread out on either side of the banks, seeping over the meadowland and low lying countryside. As the rivers near the sea, however, their beds are narrow and run through high, steep and rock-faced hills, which make no allowances for the waters in flood to spread. The natural result is that they rise, and rise quickly.

All this began to happen on the evening of the fateful Friday. In the higher parts of the moor, the brooks became small torrents and as they combined their power in the larger rivulets, so they became savage and terrible in their new found force. First saplings and the rough growth at the rivers edge were torn away; then a trapped animal, caught unawares by the swirling water in an unexpected place, and panicking, was gathered into the rushing torrent. As if in a frenzy and a trial of strength, the angry waters snatched and tore at bigger obstacles. Large trees, tremendous boulders, and anything that impeded a swift progress was carried along. The stone bridges built throughout the years, to cross what were in most cases nothing more than fording points, became choked by telegraph poles, massive trees and boulders weighing many tons each. Such stoppages proved but brief. The flood water, fast assuming the proportions of a tidal wave, was not to be hindered. In most cases the very weight of material, apart from the immense driving force behind it, swept aside the puny, man-made obstructions.

Onwards and downwards the boiling torrent raced with a velocity of twenty miles per hour. Bridges, debris, carcases of sheep, fowls, dogs, and cows and later scores of motor-cars, were gathered into its maw. Greater impetus was given—if indeed it were needed—the nearer to the coast the rivers reached, for in the last half-a-mile to the sea the West Lyn drops hundreds of feet. Rising ever higher—twenty, twenty-five, thirty, even forty feet, a veritable wall of water smashed and destroyed everything before it.

So the waters converged on Lynmouth as if through vast funnels, from two directions. As habitations became more numerous, the damage became even more ruinous. Ten-ton boulders cascading down like corks, smashed against the walls of buildings and went through them like a bullet through paper. The scour of the water undercutting the banks did its evil work under the very foundations of buildings that had remained untouched for two hundred years.

The mighty flood, lit by lightning which gave it a ghostly and terrible complexion, and accompanied by a noise as of battle and thunder, crashing, roaring and sweeping all before it, rushed out of the night . . . . . .

So the great floods came to Lynmouth!

THE ALARM IS GIVEN

Friday had been a day of rain. At midday the sky was so very heavily overcast that lights were switched on in most premises. Shortly afterwards, one observer noticed a strange phenomenon. A heavy bank of clouds, very dark and tinged with deep red and purple, seemed to creep across the sky from *West* to *East* and at the same time under that ceiling of cloud was a lower bank, which appeared to travel at a very fast rate in the opposite direction. At 1 p.m. there occurred a torrential downpour, the whole sky effect being weird and uncanny. There was a further freak storm at 5 p.m., and thereafter the rainfall was steady. Strange to say, until this last storm the rivers seemed very slow to rise, in spite of continuous rain since morning. By 5 o'clock it was dark, and whilst the rivers were certainly becoming turbulent and swollen and were rising, it was not a matter of concern. After all, any wet period made the rivers rise sometimes as much as five feet but if the water rose quickly, it fell as rapidly. The steady rain which had been endured all day was much more a subject of comment. True, the visitors were interested in the racing streams, but as none of the "locals" bothered or even evinced more than a mild interest, why should they feel alarmed?

The first intimation that the flooding was assuming serious proportions was at 7.30 p.m., when owing to damage to the canal carrying water to the Power Station, the hydro electric plant went out of action. A switch over to the diesel engine enabled a supply to be maintained to the villages until 9 o'clock, when the flywheels of the engine began picking up water and the plant had to shut down. This, of course, left the villages in complete darkness. The fact that the power remained operating so long was due to the total disregard of personal safety by Mr. C. H. Postles, the engineer in charge, and his assistant Mr. R. N. Freeman, who continued working to the last minute despite the rising flood.

The earliest reports of anything untoward were received at the Police Station at Lynton at 7.35 p.m. when Constable Pavey, who was on station duty, received a telephone call reporting that the Lynton-Simonsbath Road, between Brendon Two Gates and Scob Hill Gate, was flooded and partially washed away and therefore impassable. A few minutes later another call notified that the road on the Brendon side of Rockford was several feet under water. Routine reports were sent to the Assistant County Surveyor of Barnstaple, and Constable Harper went out to visit the immediate area. He found the water rising at Lynbridge and Barbrook, but there was no cause for alarm.

At the Police Station telephone calls began to follow one another more quickly. At 8.30 p.m. the services of the Fire Brigade were requested from Ilkerton, off the Lynton—Barnstaple Road, and above Barbrook, where a dam had burst and flooded Radsbury Farm. A fire tender was despatched to the scene. A similar request followed from Bridgeball, a hamlet a mile or so beyond Hillsford Bridge, and a second tender proceeded there, crossing Barbrook Bridge, which it was noticed was then slightly awash.

The party, consisting of six part-time firemen accompanied by Constable Harper, proceeded to Hillsford Bridge but could get no further as the roads were under water and impassable—one bridge was completely destroyed and the other damaged. Therefore, after contacting Lynton by telephone, they decided to return. It was a nightmare journey. What would normally have taken a few minutes occupied them nearly an hour, and on arrival at Barbrook Bridge it was found impossible to cross.

The river was rushing over it and little could be seen except the violent surge picked up in the headlights of the fire tender. Thus the whole party was completely isolated between the West and East Lyn rivers, as may be seen by the sketch below.

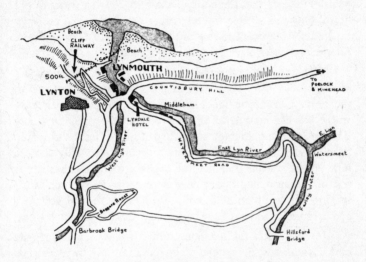

For a few minutes they remained undecided as to the next move, then cries for help were heard. Their attention was drawn to a house on the corner of the bridge by someone smashing a pane of glass. The policeman and two firemen entered the house, to find the lower portion of the premises under some five feet of water, in which a lady was floating surrounded by packing cases and bales of goods. The three men succeeded in rescuing her, and carried her to safety among neighbours.

It was then decided to try and get across the bridge, with a view to resuming communications with Lynton. Harper was secured by a rope round his waist, and closely followed by two of the firemen, commenced to make his way across. When almost a quarter of the way over, however, an increased roar of water warned those on the rope, and without further ado they hauled Harper back. Their action was only just in time, for a minute or two afterwards (at about 10.45) the bridge was smashed to pieces and carried away by the force of the onrush. It was generally agreed that the noise of the bridge giving way was not heard, only the terrible increased roar and surge, due probably to the final release of the mass of material held temporarily at bridges and other obstacles higher upstream.

Thus the plight of the party at about 11 p.m. was an augury of things to come. They were in pitch darkness and soaked to the skin, in complete ignorance of what was happening elsewhere and had an overriding anxiety about the whole situation. They made some attempt at getting dry and Harper set off to try and telephone the Police Station again. Eventually about a mile up the road he obtained the use of a telephone, but it was one of the most unpleasant calls he ever made, for due to his soaking wet condition he acted as a conductor for the electricity and received a series of uncomfortable shocks the whole time.

He was successful in making contact and was able to apprise both Lynton and Barnstaple of his position. He then returned to the firemen, one of whom in a triumph of understatement said of the occasion:—

> "*We waited around for a time drying our clothes, but Constable Harper was anxious to get to Lynmouth so we set off and eventually reached there.*"

The story of this party's further work will be taken up later.

Meanwhile, the first fire tender to be despatched had arrived at Ilkerton, but it became cut off and could not join the road at Barbrook again.

*   *   *

It is virtually impossible to give a connected story of the happenings that night. A chronological sequence fails, due to the fact that time ceased to exist for most of those concerned, with the result that any two witnesses rarely agree to within an hour about the time of any incident. To complicate matters further, there were all kinds of freak happenings. For instance, the cottages at Middleham were much further up the East Lyn river than Bevan's Cottages, which were situated close to the Lyndale Hotel, yet the latter were washed away *before* those higher up. Those highest up the river were the last to go.

At Middleham, about half-a-mile above Lynmouth but nestling under the Watersmeet Road a few feet above normal water level, was a group of ten cottages. They were situated just below an elbow bend of the stream with their backs to it, and on the night of the tragedy all were occupied. In some of them were visitors who had spent the day packing, ready for their return home on the morrow after holidays.

Mr. R. W. Ritch, occupier of one cottage, was at home that evening, as the family had intended to go to the summer show. The pouring rain, however, led them to cancel their seats. Early in the evening Mr. Ritch had noticed that the river was fairly high, but he was quite unconcerned about it.

Darkness descended very early, a fact that was well remembered for the lights had to be switched on at tea time. Once inside the house Mr. Ritch stayed there. It was his father-in-law, a visitor from Northumberland, who first showed some concern about the rapidly rising water. His interest and surprise were understandable, for he had never seen the stream anything larger than a gentle trickle. About 8.15 he had been to the back door watching the rain and returned saying: "Has anybody ever seen the river as high as this before, for it is just two feet short of being at road level!" The occupants of the house then moved upstairs to get a better view and in the short space of time that it took them, they found the river had risen a further two feet and was then *over* the road. Even then no real alarm was felt.

The water began to seep under the back door, and members of the household were then quite philosophically engaged in removing the more transportable furniture upstairs. This was about 8.30. Soon afterwards it was decided to wake the children which they did and carried them to a friend's house close by, but on higher ground.

Some of the occupants of the cottages left about 9 o'clock, when the electric lighting finally failed. That it was in their opinion a temporary move was obvious from the fact that Mr. and Mrs. G. Hicks and their daughter rolled their carpet and carried it upstairs before joining other neighbours.

In one of the ten cottages were Mr. and Mrs. W. H. Watts, aged eighty-two and seventy-two respectively, and Mr. G. Litson, aged seventy-eight years, a brother of Mrs. Watts. When the water began to rise, all three were repeatedly appealed to by neighbours to leave the house but, safely ensconced upstairs, they refused.

The occupants of all the other cottages moved out and many stayed the night at the school, which although not more than fifty or sixty yards away, was higher up the cliff side and quite safe. Others, linked arm in arm to give each other support, took the road—then several feet deep in water—down to the village.

Soon afterwards events happened with terrible rapidity. It was thought that one of the bridges which was dammed higher up the river must have collapsed, for the water rose rapidly and began to fill the cottages. The sole remaining and aged occupants must have realised their terrible position, and their agony of mind does not bear thinking about. The anxious and helpless watchers at the school saw a light burning in the bedroom which they occupied, up to midnight. Just the one flicker of light in the awful darkness, and then that light went out.

The water was now ceiling high within the houses. The rumbling, crashing and roaring had doubled in volume and it was difficult to hear anyone shouting even when standing close by. Above all—except for occasional lightning—there was a blanket of darkness, which made conditions even more terrifying. Any attempt at contacting the poor unfortunate people was out of the question.

A particularly violent roar was heard above the general tumult at 1.20 a.m. The feelings experienced by those in the safety of the school can well be imagined, for that is believed to have been the time when the houses were swept into the fury of the flood. No one saw the buildings go, some indeed refused to believe they had gone, until the first streaks of daylight revealed the terrible evidence. All that remained, by some strange chance, was one of the two gateposts of the first house and on a nearby tree a sign "Bed and Breakfast". Today, a drain is the only evidence of where ten cottages once stood. The stream in front had its bed raised by ten feet and the water is divided by a large island shoal comprising massive boulders, large trees, tree roots and silt.

Farther down, also on the Watersmeet Road, but near the stream, were the four dwellings known as Bevan's Cottages. The Rudall family occupied one of them. As was the case elsewhere, no concern was felt about the rising river until quite late in the evening. Everyone who possibly could kept within doors on such a night, and it was not until the tell-tale water began to trickle under the door that any notice was taken.

In the case of Bevan's Cottages, this was at 9.50. The front door had been bolted and barred to withstand the pressure of the water. The fact that it was appearing at the back, showed that it was surrounding the cottages but no real alarm was felt until suddenly the front door, forced by a tree or boulder, crashed open to admit a waist-deep wave. As if to synchronize, the back door flew inwards and the two surges of water met in the kitchen. There was no electric power and all witnesses agree on the feeling of impotence without light, and the deafening noise which intensified within minutes.

Mr. Rudall managed to carry a young grandson to a wall at the back, which abutted higher ground. He returned for his wife. As he staggered away neck-deep in water, he saw at the upstairs window his neighbour, Bill Richards, who called out:— 'Get us help, the houses are going." It was the last ever seen of that family. Mr. and Mrs. Richards and their two children, aged three years and three months respectively, were washed away as the houses collapsed minutes later.

Two middle-aged ladies, visitors, were also presumed drowned from these cottages. Their bodies were never recovered.

Vale Cottages was a group of three dwellings and the occupant of one of them was Mr. F. W. Bale, who returned home after duty as a traffic warden at 7.30 p.m. Even at that time he struggled home through water up to his knees but was not unduly worried, and certainly had no premonition of the tragedy to come.

It was the same story as higher up the river—water seeping through, and at 9.30 something heavy smashing open the door to let the flood surge in. This family's exit was by scrambling over the roof of a garage which abutted their cottage. It was impossible to walk up the road, so great was the force of the water.

*   *   *

The road to Lynton and Lynmouth wends its way through the hamlet of Barbrook, where in normal times the West Lyn river—some thirty feet below the level of the road—flows towards the sea. On the right-hand side, with the backs overlooking the gorge, were twelve Council houses built in 1928. From this little block twelve lives were lost and as elsewhere, fate dealt some queer blows, destroying here, saving there, with no apparent discrimination.

Three of the houses were occupied by members of the Floyd family. At that nearest to the Barbrook bridge lived Mr. and Mrs. G. Williams. Next door were Mr. T. Floyd, a postman and a Lynton Urban District councillor, his invalid wife who slept downstairs, his son Fred, aged twenty-seven, and a daughter Mrs. Bowen with her husband and two sons, aged twelve and nine years. There were also two visitors from Durham who had been given shelter for the night.

It had rained all day, and as the evening wore on, the downpour intensified. At some time after 9.30, Fred Floyd went to the kitchen and found that the river had risen up to the level of the house, some thirty feet, and became perturbed. He looked out at the front and found the water over the road. Returning to his father, he said:—"We must get mother out" and assisted by his father, he proceeded to get Mrs. Floyd off her bed. It was the last thing he ever did. With a shattering roar, the cottage was hit by the giant wave of the flood and it simply disintegrated.

One moment the house was intact with seven adults and two children within its walls; seconds afterwards it was gone, and of the nine people only one survived. This was Mr. Tom Floyd, aged sixty-three years. He remembers his son's last words:—"We must get mother out" and then seemed to be going down into a pit of water. He remembers, too, being siphoned upwards, and grabbing some masonry which proved to be the back of where his house had been. Regaining his feet, he found himself in the roadway in front of the cottages, and when being forced along by the rushing water he was caught by his daughter standing at her door a few yards along. Another astounding fact is that Floyd's dog Tim, a four-year-old Cairn terrier, also in the room with them when the building collapsed, had got to the same refuge ahead of him. With the terrific rush of water outside, the depth of that gorge and the debris being carried along, it is nothing short of a miracle that either master or dog survived.

Some idea of the awful force of the water may be gleaned from the fact that the body of nine-year-old Kenneth Bowen, who was swept away from the same house, was found under a slab in a butchers' shop in the Watersmeet Road. The body of his eleven-year-old brother has never been found.

Farther along lived Mrs. Ridd, and her eight-year-old grandson. It was about 8 o'clock on that fateful evening, when trudging up the road in the heavy rain came two Australian girls—Gwenda Oxley aged twenty-two and Joyce Hiscock, twenty-one years. Temporarily employed in London, they were on a hiking holiday in North Devon, but due to the rain had begged a lift from Blackmoor Gate. The motorist had dropped them at Barbrook and they sought shelter at the first dwelling they came to. It happened to be No. 10 Barbrook Cottages and Mrs. Ridd took them in. Later she called out to a neighbour, Mrs. Jenkins, that she had done so and expressed sympathy at the fact that the two girls were soaked to the skin.

Mr. and Mrs. Jenkins, another son-in-law and daughter of Mr. Floyd, occupied a cottage in the same row. Their first inkling of trouble was strange. The kitchen tap, instead of running clear, just gave off filthy water, so they decided to put a bath outside the front door to collect rain water. They opened the front door and together placed the bath on the step and as they let go, so it was swept away. It was the first warning they had of the water on their very doorstep. This incident shows, too, the intense darkness of the night.

One of the heroes of the occasion was sixteen-year-old Roy Williams. He was looking after his two brothers, the three being alone in a cottage in the same block. He saw the outer part of the kitchen slide into the river. Without losing his presence of mind, he rushed out to the front and instructed Morris (aged thirteen) to pass John (aged three) who was still asleep, through the window to him. This accomplished, they put John to safety in a hen house and there, incredulous though it may seem, the cackling of the incommoded hens succeeded where the tragedy of the night had failed—it woke the little fellow from his slumbers.

Strange to say, the cottages at Barbrook were not destroyed, as might be thought, by the rush of water when the bridge just above gave way. They went some time before, at about 10 o'clock, whereas the bridge was not swept away until 10.45.

It is believed that Mrs. Ridd and her grandson, hastening to safety, disappeared in the gap where the road had collapsed into the gorge. The two Australian girls were not seen at this critical time. They were drowned, but under what circumstances is not known. Their bodies were later recovered.

THE WORK OF RESCUE

It will be remembered that the crew of No. 2 Fire Tender accompanied by Constable Harper, were anxious to return to Lynmouth. They therefore retraced their course towards Hillsford Bridge and on arrival at about 1 a.m., four hours after their first attempt, found the water had receded enough to allow them to make a precarious way down the Watersmeet Road to Lynmouth. It was a formidable struggle, for large trees, roots, telegraph poles and boulders had to be moved from the path of their vehicle. Eventually they arrived as close to the village as was possible, and found a scene of indescribable desolation and confusion.

The shops and houses close to the Lyndale Hotel were flooded up to a height of about ten feet, and the terrified occupants were trapped. A veritable wall of debris was piled against the side of the hotel, and beyond was a gigantic mass of water rushing across the front of the building. Whole blocks of buildings had disappeared. There was no means of contacting the other side, so once again the party found themselves isolated. Their nine-mile nightmare journey had taken them to the very centre of the disaster.

People were crying out for help, and so the firemen commenced the work of rescue, bringing many down from upstair rooms, including one elderly lady who was paralysed. Those grim-faced men toiled unceasingly until, as far as was known, all in the immediate area were safe. It is believed that between them they brought at least thirty people to safety.

Meanwhile, Harper had scrambled up the small mountain of rubble and boulders, which was the only possible means of access to the Lyndale Hotel, and entered the building by a landing window. Thus he was the first to make contact with those who had been marooned there for five hours.

The Lyndale Hotel, known to visitors the world over, has been in the family of the present proprietor, Mr. Tom Bevan, for eighty years. On the night of the floods, there were some forty guests, beside the members of his own family and staff. Its position by the Lyndale Bridge, under which the East Lyn flowed, made it particularly vulnerable when the river changed its course. This meant that the two rivers joined at the front steps of the hotel, and the side of the building acted as a dam for the water and debris, forcing the torrent to turn aside. The hotel, therefore, had one river at the side and was in the direct path of the second. Had the flood continued for a very little while longer, there is no doubt that the building would have been entirely washed away, for nothing would have withstood much longer the vicious onslaught.

About 9 p.m. the rising East Lyn river overflowed its banks and flooded the hotel cellars. Nobody was alarmed about the occurrence and Mr. Bevan put through a telephone call asking for the services of the Fire Brigade to pump the water clear. As readers will have gathered, no machine was available. Soon afterwards, however, the West Lyn river broke its banks and isolated the hotel. Demolishing the Chapel, the Glen Fruit Shop and a garage in its rush, the debris piled up against the south side of the Lyndale, which acted as a trap for it. "Debris" is perhaps too mild a word to use, for boulders weighing up to ten tons, whole trees and silt built up a large sloping mound some thirty feet high, which reached to the landing windows.* When

---

*The fall away of the land on this corner makes it difficult to convey the correct impression by talking of first or second floors. The flood level mark afterwards showed the window to be some twenty-four feet from ground level.

the Glen Fruit Shop crashed, four people were washed against the side of the hotel and hauled to safety by those within, through the lounge and office windows.

The water quickly rose to the height of the reception hall, which by nature of the levels was well above that of the street. The guests were, therefore advised to go to the first floor. Before any attempt at salvage could be made, the water forced the doors and completely submerged the lower floor. At intervals in the hours that followed, the sixty occupants of the hotel mounted floor by floor until they were at the top of the building. Provided with rugs, blankets and eiderdowns but without light, heat, food or drink, they sat together as the interminable hours dragged by. It was an agonising period of suspense.

In the direct course of the flooded rivers and in the path of the pounding debris, the hotel received a severe battering for hours on end. The very walls seemed to rock and the groaning and straining of timbers, together with the roar of the waters, the thunder, lightning, and the whimpering of terror-stricken children was a nightmare experience, which will never be forgotten by those who were unfortunate enough to take part in it.

About midnight a fearful crash was heard above all other noises, and the building seemed to rock more violently than ever. The cause was subsequently found to be the collapse of the rear wing of the building, which included the billiard room and a number of other rooms. It was at this time that Bevan's cottages at the rear must have been washed away.

The arrival of Constable Harper coincided with the first streaks of dawn and after consultation with Mr. Bevan, it was decided to evacuate everyone from the building. They were all assisted through the landing window—still the only means of exit and entrance—and down the mound of debris to the street level, from which the waters had by then receded. Mr. Bevan afterwards paid tribute to all who shared in the gruelling experience, and said that at no time during the long vigil was there any sign of panic.

Harper was still anxious to make contact with the outside world and to bring help in. He therefore decided to make an attempt to cross to the Countisbury side. Now that the water had receded a little the parapet of the bridge seemed intact, so he straddled the stonework and crossed safely. He then made his way to the Tors Hotel, which stands on higher ground and was therefore immune. There he found some 150 people, visitors and residents alike sharing a vigil. It was then 4 a.m. but Harper borrowed a car from the hotel proprietor and with one of the staff set off up Countisbury Hill to try and make contact with Minehead. Driving conditions were awful. Fog brought visibility down to about five yards. There was moreover a thick drizzle, and bearing in mind the nature of Countisbury Hill road and the fact that he had to drive with his head out of the side window, the journey was, to say the least, hazardous. On arrival at Porlock, however, they were fortunate and found that the telephone was in order. Having made contact they returned to Lynmouth at 6 a.m.

*　　　*　　　*

To revert back to the evening before. Soon after 8 p.m. water began to penetrate all the buildings in the vicinity of Lyndale Bridge, and helpers assisted residents in an attempt to remove furniture etc. The thunder and lightning was particularly distressing at the time and people in the street, finding themselves suddenly knee deep in water began clamouring for help, some even smashing windows and crawling into shops and houses to obtain shelter. In the majority of cases, however, no sooner had they done so than the roles reversed, and the rescued became rescuers. In some instances as the level of the water rose in the downstairs rooms and the staircases were cut off, attempts were made to make holes in the ceiling in order to get to the floor above. When this was found to be impossible, outside help was employed and scores were rescued in the nick of time.

The Glen Fruit Shop occupied a position close to the Lyndale Hotel, where the coach park is now situated. With adjoining buildings it received the full brunt of the West Lyn river when it changed direction and swept everything in its way to destruction. Some idea of the colossal havoc may be gleaned from the fact that next morning about thirty feet of debris including fifteen ton boulders were piled up in the area.

About 9 o'clock a rush of water came from the East Lyn direction (from the back of the Lyndale Hotel towards the foot of Lynmouth hill). It forced open the doors of one premises and appeared to reach the ceiling in a moment. The windows were wrenched out and the groaning of timber seemed to sound a death-knell. After the first wave the water receded a little and the poor bewildered, trapped victims found themselves with water at waist-height. It was but a temporary respite, however, for it gradually rose again.

The people in the Lyndale Hotel seemed so close (but the width of the roadway) but could, of course, hear nothing amid the awful noise. Visibility too was restricted only to glimpses obtained as lightning flashed.

Mrs. B. Pavey, who was visiting friends at the fruit shop, was caught by the flood. Accompanied by her nephew, Michael Spry of London, a lad of sixteen years of age, they attempted to leave the shop when the water began to rise rapidly, but they got no further than outside the door when they were swept off their feet by the surge of the flood. To avoid being carried away, they grasped the handrail outside and hung on. The youngster realised that Mrs. Pavey could not hold on much longer and courageously changed positions with her, so that he took the full force of the water on the end of the rail. He then tried to get over to the Lyndale hotel for a rope. He got to the hotel window and hammered on it, to let them know that he was there. At the same time two other people managed to get to the hotel window. To rescue Mrs. Pavey a man held by those inside let his legs trail into the racing water outside the window, and Mrs. Pavey was able to grasp them and in such a manner was pulled to safety. A few minutes later there was no sign of the rail to which they had been clinging.

* * *

At the Lynton Police Station, when the first calls were received early in the evening, Constable Pavey was on duty. He maintained contact by telephone with Lynmouth until relieved by Constable Earle, Lynton's senior Constable, who reported for duty. Police Constable Earle arranged for the evacuation of all at Lynbridge and then collected ropes and ladders and proceeded to Lynmouth, where he organised a party and carried on the work of rescue. The river at the foot of Lynmouth Hill had burst its banks, and was then some thirty feet wide. People were leaving the Lyn Valley Hotel, and together with those who had taken shelter in the entertainment Pavilion round by the Cliff Railway, were conducted to the foot of Lynmouth Hill to make their way to Lynton.

Constables Earle and Pavey worked ceaselessly with rescue parties and made every endeavour to maintain communication with the outside. Throughout the night the latter worked without respite, in spite of the fact that he had no knowledge of the whereabouts of his wife, except that she was in the flood area. Her rescue has already been mentioned.

Meanwhile the greatest bravery was being shown in every corner of the little town. People in all walks of life were responding to the occasion and working in small parties, rescuing and carrying to safety those who were marooned or in danger.

Just before midnight an appeal for assistance was made by Supt. West at Barnstaple Police Headquarters, to the Officer

Commanding the Amphibious Warfare Experimental establishment at Fremington, near Barnstaple. The position as it was then known was explained, and a DUKW with an officer and crew of fourteen men, was immediately despatched. While it was hoped that the vehicle would be able to cross the flooded road at Barbrook, a police guide in a patrol car was stationed at Dean Steep in case it was impossible to get through. As events proved, it was a wise precaution, for even the "Duck" was unable to negotiate the floods as it neared Barbrook. Inspector Burgess and Sergeant Edwards, manning the police car, therefore decided to make an attempt to guide them to Lynmouth via the old coach route—Lydiate Lane—which leads from the main road above Dean Steep down to Lynton.

The route was no more than a typical Devon lane with a gradient in parts of one in three-and-a-half. Moreover, for most of its length it was a deep cut lying some five feet below the fields on either side. For nine months in the year it is a treacherous, wet and muddy surface, and until fairly recent years it was used as a motor-cycle test hill. It may well be imagined, therefore, the task that faced the team on this particular night. The fact that the Army vehicle was thirty-one feet long and eight feet three inches wide and the lane rarely more than nine feet, gives some indication of the enormous difficulties and hazards which were undertaken and overcome.

This little force arrived at Lynton at 2 a.m., and scarcely stopping for a cup of tea, the men led by Constable Pavey proceeded down into Lynmouth, where without delay they joined in the work of rescue. When it became light they constructed a temporary footbridge of planks and ladders across the West Lyn, which made it possible for them to evacuate some thirty people to safety. Later, at the request of the Police they moved to Barbrook to effect some temporary repairs to the roadway there.

Meanwhile an officer had made a reconnaissance and reported back to Fremington stating that tools, ropes, scaffolding, transport and equipment for bridges, together with more troops should be got ready as they would be needed.

The extent of the disaster was, of course, becoming appreciated and simultaneously with the appeal to Fremington, the R.A.F. at Chivenor were asked for help. They, too, started off at once bringing lorries and equipment. The Police had also asked for help elsewhere, and it was immediately given by men of the 264 Scottish Beach Brigade, T.A., who were in camp at Braunton.

The headquarters of the County Police, Middlemoor, Exeter. had been first contacted with a routine report on the first flooding. Owing to the breakdown of communications, however, the full details did not reach Headquarters until 4.30 a.m. on Saturday. Immediately steps were taken to send reinforcements from all parts of Devon.

*   *   *

Under normal circumstances, the West Lyn river ran under the bridge at the foot of Lynmouth Hill between the West Lyn Cafe and the Lyn Valley hotel, where it joined at a right angle the East Lyn on the last few hundred yards to the sea. The West Lyn, as has already been explained, changed course when the bridge became blocked, and joined its companion higher up. Both greatly distended, they overflowed the banks, and together swept through Lynmouth Street, forming a channel through which the heavy debris was driven, pounding on the walls, finding the weaker places and battering its way through.

All the buildings on the left-hand side of the street were veritable traps when the water rose, for they were built into the cliff which rises steeply behind. There were no rear exits, except those that led back again to the main street. It was in this area particularly that men toiled through the night with ladders and ropes, getting away to safety scores of people who had been trapped. It was the appalling suddenness of events that seemed to shock those who were involved.

When the lights failed at the Pavilion where the concert party were performing, the show closed down. The audience, reaching the street, were astounded to find the roads covered with water to a considerable depth. Many people avoided Lynmouth Street and ascended Mars Hill, but a group of seven lady holiday-makers linked arms and began to make their way through flooded Lynmouth Street. A Miss Cherry, aged fifty-six years, of Highgate, London, was on the extreme left nearest the crumbling river bank. As they approached the Lyn Valley Hotel she stumbled and in just those few seconds, before her companions realised what had happened, she was washed away. Her body was recovered at Clovelly many weeks later. Undoubtedly taken unawares in the same manner, three residents—two women and a man—lost their lives in the same vicinity and under like circumstances.

Supt. C. A. Durman of the St. John Ambulance Brigade, was at this time in Lynmouth Street where he had been directed in order to evacuate an elderly lady, who had been marooned by the floods. As he was endeavouring to turn his ambulance, two ladies came floating down in the water. One of them managed to grab a wheel of the ambulance and he rescued her. The other, believed to have been Miss Cherry, was washed away.

At the Lyn Valley Hotel on Lynmouth Street, fifty people found themselves trapped as the roadway became a rushing river. It had been the same story in this hotel as in others, and guests suddenly found themselves on the first floor looking down at a veritable wall of water, which had crashed open doors and windows. The staff lit candles when the electric lighting failed, and about 10.45 they began to think about evacuation. Soon afterwards the tower of the hotel, which stood against the river bank, crashed into the flood. It was this which probably attracted the attention of the rescue party, who then concentrated their activities on the building. It was a hazardous undertaking by reason of the fact that the only possible means of exit was by some form of bridging from the first floor of the hotel, across to the rescuers on the cliff at the rear.

The rescue party, including Dr. M. P. Nightingale, Medical Officer for the town, who did grand work that night, climbed down the cliff at the back of the premises and bridged Granny's Lane to the rear window ledge of the hotel with a ladder. A torrent was rushing underneath and the greatest care had to be exercised. Each person had to be roped for additional safety, and all this mid a turmoil of sound and in complete darkness. In this manner all the occupants of the building, numbering about fifty, were brought to safety. The candles which had provided the only illumination were left burning, and cast a weird ghostly flicker over the scene.

When this rescue operation was completed, the party moved along and repeated the manoeuvre behind the Bath Hotel, which lies higher up the street towards the harbour. This was in the early hours of the morning. Again a climb down the cliff side was necessary, and reaching the roof of a shop, a rope was thrown across the street which was then a raging river. The rope was secured to a lamp post on one side and on the other to a bedroom in a house, Prior's Cottage. Eight people were rescued from there and as they were taken across the street the water was shoulder high. The rescued included a lady of eighty-five years, for whom earlier in the evening an ambulance was requisitioned but could not get near enough to be put to any use. The old lady survived her ordeal.

In the early hours of the morning after the rescues at the Lyn Valley Hotel and the Bath Hotel, the sole remaining contact to Lynton was by the telephone of Mr. S. C. Willshere, whose fruiterer's shop, by reason of the fact that it was in the middle of the street and flanked on either side by buildings, escaped much of the pounding suffered by those less protected. He gave what was to all intents and purposes a running commentary to those at the top of the hill. He explained that the water was racing down Lynmouth Street, had entered his shop and was above the counter, and in a cool, calm and collected manner, went on telling the rescue parties that although there seemed no immediate danger, people were calling for help all round. He advised them to collect ropes and ladders, in order to effect a rescue as and when they could get near enough to do so. At intervals he rang up to reassure those who were anxiously waiting above, that the water was going down and finally, reminded them that when they did arrive to bring some cigarettes, for he had smoked his last! This remaining telephone link ceased about 2 a.m.

Mr. Pedder, Lynmouth's postmaster, was not so fortunate. He was endeavouring to remove Post Office papers to safety and became trapped in a small office which opened off the shop and had no other exit. His schoolboy son, showing great presence of mind, smashed the skylight of the office and hoisted his father clear, undoubtedly saving his life in doing so.

The disaster made clear the part that Civil Defence organisations can play in peace time as well as in war. This was amply demonstrated by Mr. W. H. Tall, who was the Civil Defence Controller designate for Lynton. Immediately he heard of the flood, he visited Lynmouth and having obtained a first hand picture of the situation, returned and established a control centre at the Valley of Rocks Hotel, which incidentally was the only building with emergency lighting. He then collected volunteers for various duties and returned to the stricken area to assist in the rescue operations, and later requested that Rest Centres be opened. After the initial period had passed, Mr. Tall continued to work with very little rest for several days. He proved himself a resourceful organiser, and most helpful to all who approached him for help or advice.

The Rising Sun Hotel is the first building of a number on Mars Hill, which rises very steeply up to the corner of Lynmouth Hill. Except for Lynmouth Street, it is the only way of getting to the hill. The little terrace outside the hotel is about six feet above the road level. Mr. Hardman, the proprietor, first had forebodings when the pleasure and fishing boats normally moored opposite his hotel, broke away soon after 8 o'clock. The water rose first above the roadway and then the six feet to the door, but that proved to be the top flood level and at no time did the water get inside.

The hotel seemed to bear a charmed existence that night, and it was only afterwards realised that it was saved by the Turbal Rock, a projection of virgin rock which protrudes behind Manor Cottage and proved a breakwater for both the cottage and the hotel. The Beach Hotel and the Lifeboat Station on the other side of the rock projection were washed away completely.

The Rising Sun was open house for all assisting that night. In addition to the twenty-six guests staying there, a further twenty-five including those who had arrived when the concert party closed down in the nearby Pavilion spent the night there in safety.

Constable Pavey standing at the entrance to the Rising Sun and looking up Lynmouth Street, saw the Beach Hotel collapse and disintegrate into the flood water. What was more astounding, however, was that while he was watching, the double doors of a garage on the opposite side of the road gradually opened without any human agency. They just seemed to swing slowly outwards and a Wolseley car backed steadily into the roadway. Just as if there was a human being at the wheel, if kept straight in the centre of the road. It maintained this course for fifty yards, then swerved into a building, got hooked by its rear bumper and came to a standstill in the swirling water. Perhaps the most fantastic part of all was that the registration number of the car was END.

When the Beach Hotel disappeared, there were a dozen cars in the Bath Hotel car park close by. When some of the rescue party went into the Rising Sun to make a telephone call all was in darkness, but when they came out some time later, all the car lights were glaring on to the rushing water. The explanation was, of course, that the water had risen, shorted the electrical systems and had acted as an automatic time switch.

Despite the stark tragedy that stalked on every hand, there were some flashes of typical British humour recorded. For instance, the brawny rescuer who, carrying an elderly lady down a ladder, was heard to say as they reached safety:— "Blinkin' funny ain't it lady, some people get paid £10 a week in a circus for doin' things like this!"

Some who were watching on the roads above flood level that night have strange experiences to relate. One group on the Countisbury Hill side were watching the waters as they were lit by flashes of lightning—in itself an awe-inspiring sight. Suddenly the headlights of a car came into view, travelling, it seemed, down the Watersmeet Road. While the watchers were transfixed, the car seemed to glide into the waters with the lights still shining but turning to a weird green. Like the eyes of a huge submarine monster they raced on seemingly for quite a distance and then, as suddenly as they had come into view they were extinguished leaving a chill of horror to those who witnessed the occurrence.

There were many amazing happenings. One house was almost razed to the ground, yet safe and sound on the remaining table was a dish of eggs and not one of them even cracked. In Barbrook, a cabinet of china fell off the wall during one of the many shocks sustained by the building. When picked up next morning not a piece of china was even chipped. A similar case was in a house on the Watersmeet Road, where a china cupboard crashed and everything inside was smashed—everything, except a set of very delicate thin-stemmed wine glasses.

A PRE-FLOOD PICTURE. The East Lyn joined the West Lyn at a point roughly in the centre of the picture and ran between the cafe and Bevan's Hotel.

THE SCENE WHEN THE WATERS SUBSIDED AT THE BOTTOM OF LYNMOUTH HILL. Note the massive tree root; the centre window of the Lyndale Hotel was the only means of access to the Countisbury side until the thirty-foot pile of debris seen in the picture, was removed.

THE SAME SCENE AS PREVIOUS PAGE WHEN A COMMENCEMENT HAD BEEN MADE AT CLEARANCE. The Army engineers were at work on the temporary bridge.

(51)

THE COUNTY COUNCIL STAFF SURVEYING FOR THE COURSE OF THE WEST LYN.
The gap on the right was the tower of Lyn Valley Hotel. Note the enormous boulder in
the foreground. Comparisons can be made by the size of the men in the picture.

GIANT BOULDERS LITTERED THE BEDS OF THE STREAMS

SOME OF THE AFTERMATH. Note the car at left foreground

AT THE FOOT OF LYNMOUTH HILL. Note the height of the debris

VIEW FROM LYNDALE BRIDGE (Foot of Countisbury Hill)

THE RIVER BACK TO ITS NORMAL FLOW BEFORE THE BULLDOZERS STARTED WORK

ALL THAT WAS LEFT OF THE HOUSES AT BARBROOK

THE DEBRIS OF WRECKED HOMES AND BUILDINGS

THIS AERIAL PICTURE SHOWS THE SCENE AFTER THE FLOODS HAD RECEDED

IT LITTERED THE FORESHORE OVER AN ENORMOUS AREA AFTER THE FLOOD

Note height of silt against shops in the immediate foreground.   Lynmouth Hill right.

EVACUATION SCENE AT PROSPECT CORNER

LYNMOUTH STREET THE MORNING AFTER

THE ENORMOUS GULLIES SCOURED OUT BY THE WATERS IN A DEVONSHIRE ROAD. This one is only six feet deep, some were as much as eighteen feet.

Three Pictures which illustrate the damage.

No wonder it reminded people of air raids.

THE BAILEY BRIDGE ERECTED BY THE ARMY TO REPLACE THE OLD HILLSFORD BRIDGE

TYPICAL OF THE MOTOR-CARS WHICH LITTERED THE FORESHORE

A SIXTEEN-WHEEL 20-TON ARMY TRAILER THAT WENT OVER THE TOP

ARMY, POLICE AND CIVILIANS ASSIST IN EVACUATION

LITTLE STREAMS TURN KILLERS

The wreckage of a town lies strewn across its beach

Firemen saved 14 from water

REPORT TO CABINET TO

HOTELS, HOUSE, CARS SWEPT A

Devon mountains were 'reservoir of death,' says Mr. Isaac Foot

TROOPS OUT IN 250 SQUARE MILES FLOOD AREA

Appeal made for 100 caravans

Swift flood aid by Government is expected

120,000 TONS OF DEBRIS THREAT TO LYNMOUTH

Gifts, Large And Small, Swell Fund

Community spirit shown in West flood area

WORK AS WELL AS

Floo faces disas

Holidaymakers families wait and hope

Biggest danger is peak tide

AS the known death the Devon flood dis rose last night, rain fell and the sky was "black.

SOME OF THE PRESS HEADINGS, 1952

(63)

ALL THAT WAS LEFT OF THE BEACH HOTEL

THE EAST LYN FLOWS DOWN THE LOVELY WATERSMEET VALLEY. NOTE NEW
RIVER WALLS

THE NEW BRIDGE AT THE FOOT OF COUNTISBURY HILL. THE FORMER BRIDGE MAY BE SEEN ON PAGE 56.

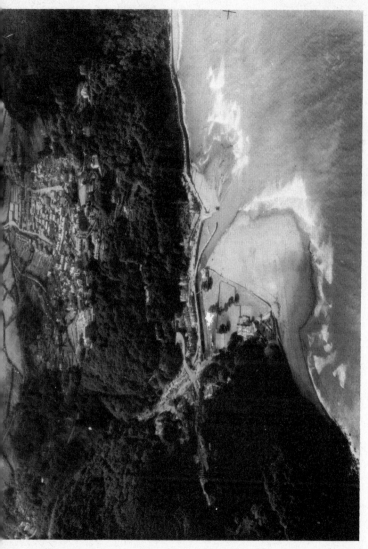

A SPLENDID AERIAL VIEW OF LYNMOUTH with Lynton spread out 500 feet above.
Reproduced by courtesy of L. A. Pope

MR. R. B. CARNEGIE (DEVON COUNTY SURVEYOR) WHO WAS AWARDED THE C.B.E. He was in charge of the clearance and rehabilitation.

LIEUT.-COLONEL R. R. M. BACON (CHIEF CONSTABLE OF DEVON) WHO WAS RESPONSIBLE FOR THE SPLENDID WORK OF THE POLICE.

THE COUNTESS ELDON, O.B.E. Vice
President of the Devon Red Cross.

MRS. E. A. STANLEY, M.B.E. who was in
charge of the Emergency Feeding.

MRS. D. SLATER, O.B.E. Chairman, Lynton
Urban District Council.

POLICE CONSTABLE DEREK HARPER WHO
WAS AWARDED THE GEORGE MEDAL FOR
HIS WORK

POLICE CONSTABLE J. H. EARLE and POLICE CONSTABLE S. H. J. PAVEY OF
LYNTON, BOTH OF WHOM RECEIVED THE BRITISH EMPIRE MEDAL
(CIVIL DIVISION).

Supt. F. W. DONEY
In charge Traffic
Department, Devon
Constabulary.

Mr. L. RIDGE
Town Clerk, Lynton
Urban District
Council.

MR. TOM FLOYD AND HIS DOG TIM

FIELD-MARSHAL SIR WILLIAM SLIM WITH THE COUNTY SURVEYOR

TEDDY WAS SOME CONSOLATION

AFTER ONE MONTH. A car park on the site of the demolished buildings. Compare with picture on pages 50 and 51

WHEN THE FLOODS HAD RECEDED

BEACH HOTEL

The dotted line shows where the road had been. Mars Hill, only alternative route, on right

THE LYNTON FIREMENT WHO RECEIVED THE QUEEN'S COMMENDATION FOR BRAVE CONDUCT

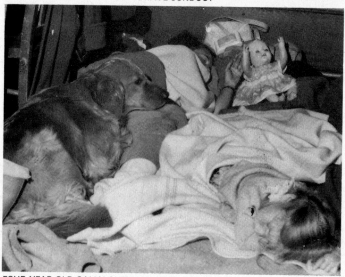

FOUR-YEAR-OLD SALLY OXENHAM WITH HER DOG, MINSTREL, ON GUARD AT THE REST CENTRE

FIELD-MARSHAL SIR WILLIAM SLIM BEING GREETED BY MAJOR-GENERAL C. L. FIRBANK, ON HIS ARRIVAL BY HELICOPTER AT LYNTON CAR PARK

THE RT. HON. HAROLD MACMILLAN AT THE COUNCIL OFFICES. Also in the picture are Mrs. D. Slater (Chairman, Lynton U.D.C.), Mr. E. J. Pedder, Lieut.-Col. R. M. M. Bacon and Mr. S. C. Willishere.

The
Great Clean
Up

Operation
''King Canute''

Operation
''Estuary''

THE SCENE AT THE FUNERAL SERVICE

THE CARAVAN CAMP AT HOLMAN PARK

H.R.H. THE DUKE OF EDINBURGH ASCENDING TO LYNTON BY THE CLIFF RAILWAY DURING HIS VISIT IN OCTOBER 1952

THE PEACEFUL SCENE AS MILLIONS KNEW IT WITH THE RHENISH TOWER, WHICH DISINTEGRATED BEFORE THE ONRUSH OF THE WATERS.

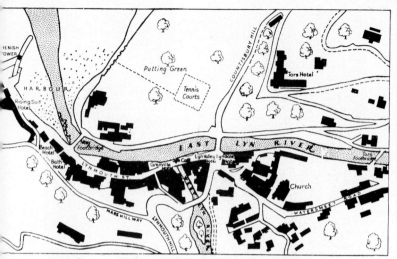

PLAN OF LYNMOUTH BEFORE THE FLOOD

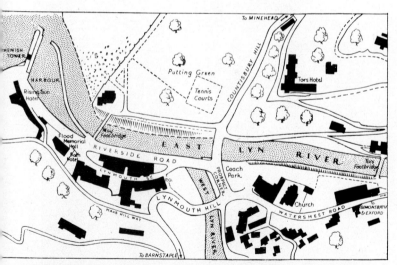

LYNMOUTH AS IT IS TODAY. COMPARISON WITH PLAN ABOVE SHOWS
BUILDINGS WHICH DISAPPEARED. NOTE ALSO ALTERED COURSE OF THE WEST
LYN AND INCREASED WIDTH OF BOTH EAST AND WEST LYN RIVERS.

A NEW FOOTBRIDGE. THE FORMER ONE (REMAINS IN THE PICTURE ON PAGE 64) HAD BEEN WASHED AWAY.

THE LYNDALE HOTEL BEFORE IT WAS DEMOLISHED

A TEMPORARY HAVEN

LYNMOUTH AS IT WAS BEFORE THE FLOOD

THE FORESHORE AFTER THE DELUGE

WHEN THE DAWN CAME

The scene that met the eye next morning defies description. It was awe inspiring and spectacular. Except for the surrounding hills the whole landscape had changed, and it is little wonder that those who knew Lynmouth well, failed to recognise it from the pictures which appeared in the newspapers.

At the bottom of Lynmouth Hill, the road had curved to join the main street and Lyndale Bridge had entirely disappeared, and where the remains of the bridge stood, there was a wide gap measuring some seventy-five feet. The trickle of a stream a few feet wide had changed to a rushing torrent that had risen by twenty feet. A chapel, shops and houses had entirely disappeared; others were so badly damaged that they were likely to fall down at any moment. Over the whole area were great boulders, trees, timber, telegraph poles, crushed and mangled motor-cars, iron girders, the remnants of household furniture and bedding, a crumpled bicycle and a thousand and one other reminders of the homes that were complete, until the day before. Gazing down with sightless eyes from a precarious position at the top of a tree, was a little sodden rag doll much the worse for wear, but it served to show the height to which the waters had risen.

The area where the East and West Lyn rivers made junction, had been completely submerged, it is estimated, by 100,000 tons of boulders, which cascaded down with the flood like corks. Boulders, debris and trees had built up to a depth in some places of over twenty-five feet. Each of the many bridges higher up the streams had formed their own dams and then as one by one they gave with the enormous pressure, they simply forced the next one in their path. Huge sections of masonry, all that was left of some of the bridges, could be seen on the streets and foreshore. In its final surge to the sea, the West Lyn by-passed the bridge at Prospect Corner and joined the East Lyn at the Lyndale Hotel.

There were no means of access to the other side of the river. The course of Lynmouth Street could still be traced by the buildings that remained, but there was a covering of many feet of silt and boulders—massive boulders weighing anything up to ten tons—all over the roadway. Here again houses and hotels had disappeared practically without trace. At intervals and in the most unexpected places, were the bloated carcases of animals, washed down from the higher parts of the river.

Round the harbour the scene was just as unfamiliar. The Rhenish Tower, which must have figured in millions of holiday snapshots, had disappeared. The mouth of the river seemed ten times its normal width, and half-a-mile out to sea were hundreds of trees just standing upright, supported by their enormous roots, just as they had been carried down in the flood when they had been snatched from the banks of the river. For a mile out to sea the water was a dirty mud colour. As the tide receded, motor-cars, pounded and crushed to compact parcels of twisted scrap, were brought to view all over the estuary.

The enormous strength of the scour of the waters may be gauged from the fact that prior to the final surge which deposited the masses of debris over everything, partly filled five hundred gallon petrol tanks buried four feet underground, outside a garage in Lynmouth Street, were uprooted from their foundations and simply swept away. No trace of them has ever been found.

Though the incredible destruction stunned the mind, here and there details stood out. Here was a cistern hanging on the wall next to the wash basin—the rest of the room, even the roof had completely disappeared. This was typical. A whole cottage had gone, yet the wooden gate still swung crazily on its hinges. Adhering to the only remaining wall of a cafe was a shelf, and the tins were still stacked neatly on it. Elsewhere was a coal bin high up on the wall, which showed it must have been on the first floor. The coal and shovel were still intact, but nothing else remained of the house. Clinging precariously to a counter was a shop till, with 3s. 7d.—the last sale rung up the night before, probably for a packet of cigarettes—still showing.

Up the Watersmeet Road and along the course of the East Lyn river were similar effects of the disaster. Whole blocks of cottages had vanished completely and massive trees seemed as if they were growing in the centre of an angry sea.

For miles around, scenes of destruction were everywhere obvious. Road surfaces had disappeared and deep gullies had been scoured at the sides of the Devonshire lanes, as if dug by a trench excavator. These gullies varied from five to as much as eighteen feet deep. No less than twenty-eight bridges (public and private) had been entirely destroyed or seriously damaged. Over the whole scene of devastation that met the eye that morning, there was a something at first indefinable, but gradually it was realised that the stench which pervaded the scene was due to the total destruction of the town's sewerage system.

In a few hours the painstaking work of man built up over the years had been entirely swept away, as if it had never existed. Roads, sewers, water mains, electricity, telephones—all had gone when nature asserted itself.

Then the stricken onlookers became aware that there was a death-roll.

* * *

The evacuation of Lynmouth commenced with the first streaks of daylight. The first of the inhabitants and visitors began to trek slowly up the hill on foot. Later, as described elsewhere, a lorry, then a bus and other vehicles including a St. John ambulance, assisted in carrying the aged and infirm up to Lynton.

Constable Pavey had already enlisted the help of the school-boys, who went from door to door to all the houses in Lynton, asking residents if they could take in some of the homeless people.

This was the real start of the information bureau which was opened at the Town Hall. In next to no time the bureau grew out of all proportion and did amazing work, until a week or so later its services were no longer required.

The Rest Centre at Jubilee Hall was opened by the Rev. Souttar, Mrs. Nightingale, Mrs. Earle, and Mr. Jarvis. In addition there were many individuals who became alive to the position at the time of the crisis, and from midnight onwards threw open their premises to all who were homeless.

The seven hundred or so people cut off on the Somerset side were conveyed to Minehead, where the authorities and residents opened Rest Centres and did all in their power to make them comfortable.

All day long the exodus continued. Frequently people reached Lynton expecting to find friends or relatives, only to be disappointed and to return immediately in an attempt to find, or glean news of the missing. One of the last to leave was an old gentleman who refused to be shaken by the water in spite of the pressure brought to bear upon him by various officials. At last he consented to go, saying:—"The floods didn't worry me, but when that blasted Scotsman started his blasting I thought I had better be going." His forthright language referred, of course, to the dynamiting being carried out by Mr. Carnegie's workman. By Saturday night everyone had left—everyone that the officials knew about! It was with some surprise next morning that workers discovered the two maiden ladies living in cottages on the Waters-meet Road, still in residence. They were sole guardians of a dead village.

The ladies were the Misses Mary and Alice Crocombe. The former was seventy-nine years of age, ten years senior to her sister. They occupied separate cottages which stood on high ground built into the cliff, and were reached from the roadway by a small flight of stone steps. It had been, to use their own description, "a rough old day", and so they went to bed at 9 p.m. They slept soundly and it was given to few to have the experience and receive the shock which they did next morning when looking out of the window—for the first time they had an uninterrupted view of the sea. The water was practically level with their door step, and the two cottages which the night before had been opposite them had completely disappeared. No wonder, again to use their own term, "they thought they had gone potty".

However, undeterred, they carried on in their normal manner. They had food, there was water at the spring a hundred yards up the road, they had bread and they had milk. The little cooking they required was done on a spirit stove. The failure of the lighting did not worry them because they went to bed early anyhow, and so they just carried on. They noted with amusement the concern of all and sundry for them when they were "rediscovered."

As the food and sanitation position became more difficult, they methodically made their own arrangements to stay with friends up at Lynton and intended to leave on the Tuesday. The sappers, however, were dynamiting all round them on the Monday and began to feel some concern—a feeling certainly not shared by the ladies themselves. It was under the greatest pressure that they were at last persuaded to have a ride up the hill a day in advance of their own time-table. They were away from their homes altogether six weeks, and were among the most willing of the residents to return directly the officials said they could do so.

*   *   *

Constable Pavey contacted his headquarters at Barnstaple about 10.30 on Friday evening, where Superintendent West—in charge of the A Division covering the area—immediately took steps to contact local military commanders. The next day an Information Bureau was set up and Post Office engineers installed additional lines for this purpose at Barnstaple Police Station. At 8 o'clock on Sunday morning the following message was broadcast over the National network:—

> "*In connection with the flooding at Lynmouth a Missing Persons Bureau has been opened in Barnstaple, where there is an incomplete list of persons known to be safe. With a view to completing this list of such persons as were in Lynton and Lynmouth at the time of the flood and who are now safe, people are asked to communicate with the Devon Constabulary at Barnstaple by telephone numbers 3022 and 3023.*"

Somewhat naturally this announcement, coupled with the publicity given by the National and overseas press, produced a deluge of enquiries. By the end of the first day something like five hundred incoming calls were dealt with, and they did not fall far below that figure daily for a week. Anxious relatives and friends telephoned from all over the country, and even farther afield. Calls were received from places as far apart as Belfast, Edinburgh, the Hebrides, the Isle of Man—and even France and the United States.

To supply the data for this bureau, the local force at Lynton, consisting of a Sergeant and three Constables, and assisted by the Local Authority, was concentrated in compiling a register of those people known to have left the area and those still remaining. In this way it was possible for those at Barnstaple to relieve the anxiety of at least sixty per cent of the callers.

Meanwhile the Chief Constable, Colonel R. R. M. Bacon, had decided to stay on the scene of action. There were many surprises when highly placed officials enquired for the Chief Constable of Devon and were directed to a prominent figure in the midst of the turmoil, working with the police but dressed in old flannel trousers and a sports coat. It was a fine example to all concerned.

Sergeant A. V. Burnard, who was on leave at the time of the happening, endeavoured to return to duty on Friday night, but could get no nearer to Lynmouth than Dean Steep. In the weeks that followed, he proved a one-man Enquiry Bureau by reason of his special knowledge of local conditions.

Lynton Police Station was never built for such an emergency, and within a few hours it was packed to capacity. Even the cells were converted into offices.

INTO ACTION

At 7.15 on Saturday morning Mr. R. B. Carnegie, the County Surveyor, was telephoned at his home and apprised of the position. He departed for Lynton right away and by 9.30 was in consultation with Mrs. D. Slater, the Chairman of the Council. Mrs. Slater has said that after a few minutes with the County Surveyor, his calm and resourceful manner had a soothing effect and he was as good as his word.

He immediately advised her that an emergency meeting of the Council should be called and suggested 12 noon, by which time he promised to have an appreciation of the position to put before them. He at once issued instructions to all the North Devon area, and lorries were sent to collect personnel and equipment. The men came from Torrington, Barnstaple, Ilfracombe, South Molton, Topsham, from the quarries and the four quarters of Devon. By 12 o'clock a hundred county council workmen were employed on the clearance of Lynmouth, in addition to two hundred others dispersed at strategic points over the flood area.

There was a tense and dramatic atmosphere in the Council Chamber of the Lynton Town Hall, when Mrs. D. Slater commenced the first of many emergency meetings convened to discuss the disaster. There were but three absentees in the ranks of the local Councillors—Tom Floyd, who had lost six members of his family the night before, and Tom Bevan, who had spent a night with fifty visitors on the top floor of his hotel, while thousands of tons of boulders and debris had battered against it. Councillor Harry Litson, aged fifty-three, was also missing. He was last seen the night before going back to help and was subsequently drowned, it is believed while engaged in the work of rescue.

Several of the members were weary-eyed with fatigue from their all-night efforts. The Medical Officer of Health, Dr. M. P. Nightingale, had spent a night of great service in Lynmouth with his people. The Surveyor, Mr. A. F. Gibbs, had made ceaseless efforts to retain communications and public services.

At the words "Madam Chairman and gentlemen, this is a National disaster" spoken by Mr. Carnegie, there was a murmur —not of approval but of consent, and putting their own troubles in the background they braced their shoulders and set to work with a will to deliberate on the best measures to relieve the distress of their fellows, and to bring order out of chaos.

Another meeting was held on Sunday when Earl Fortescue, Lord Lieutenant of the County, and Lady Fortescue; Brigadier C. H. M. Peto, Member of Parliament for North Devon; Lieut-Colonel R. R. M. Bacon, Chief Constable of Devon; Major General C. L. Firbank, General Officer Commanding South Western District, and others who were to play such an important part in the coming weeks, were present. By their clear-sighted decisions at that first meeting, they laid the foundations of the splendid work of clearance and rehabilitation which was to follow.

The Lynton Urban District Council, similar to all Local Councils of a small Urban District, consists of professional men and tradesmen, elected as the representatives of the people. The Lynton Urban District Council is to some extent unique, as it embraces not only the town of Lynton but the twin village of Lynmouth lying six hundred feet below at sea level, in addition to a large rural area. The combined population in the winter is but 2,100 with a total of eight hundred dwellings, of which three hundred were in Lynmouth. The total product of a penny rate was £76.

In the four weeks that followed no local authority could have worked more swiftly than did Lynton's. Mr. L. Ridge, the Clerk of the Council, with that wisdom general to Clerks of Councils, shepherded his Council along the well defined path of Local Government Constitution. Standing Orders were occasionally overlooked, but then ordinary Standing Orders do not cover a disaster of such magnitude. Red tape restrictions and frustrations were brushed aside without ceremony. Mrs. Slater gave a ruling. A murmur of approval, and the minute book recorded yet another decision made possible by the democratic way of life of the British people.

Mr. Ridge, who was on holiday when the disaster occurred, returned immediately and next day called a further meeting of the Council, which was attended by Sir John Shelley (Chairman of the County Council), Devon County officials, heads of the various departments concerned, and as a result Mr. Carnegie was given full authority to co-ordinate and complete the temporary phase of reconstruction of roads, bridges, sewers, water and all services. He had power to proceed regardless of the multiplicity of forms and Standing Orders, which in normal times tend to clog and strangle swift action. Events proved that without this mandate progress would not have been nearly as rapid. In this connection, tribute is due to Sir John Shelley, who authorised the County Surveyor to go ahead with whatever work he considered necessary, taking upon himself the responsibility of the County Council's later approval. In the same way the Clerk of the County Council, Mr. H. G. Godsall, was to be responsible for the clerical and legal aspects, and Brigadier C.H.M. Peto, Member of Parliament for North Devon, took charge of the Welfare Services in the early stages.

Meanwhile men of the County Council staff had started work. They commenced clearing where the roads had been, freeing the water courses and the channels leading to the bridges, or what was left of them.

Health Visitors and District Nurses worked in the Rest Centres and Sanitary Inspectors installed emergency sanitary accommodation for the workmen, firemen, police and other workers. Temporary repairs were made to broken drains and sewers. The Medical Officer asked for extra sanitary inspectors and two loaned by Torquay Borough Council came to assist Mr. Gibbs, the Lynton Surveyor and Sanitary Inspector. Their speed of action brought dividends, for the people who remained in the area suffered no effects to their health, which might well have been the case.

By Sunday morning the number of men in Lynmouth had been increased to one hundred and fifty, and whilst Mr. Carnegie was the first to appreciate that there was little the men could do pending the arrival of outside help and heavy equipment, the effect of the one hundred and fifty men working as if their lives depended on it, had an extremely good effect on morale and did much to hearten the residents of Lynmouth.

All day Sunday men and women toiled as if possessed. The Welfare Services came in, troops arrived; there were representatives of all the essential Services so that by Monday morning the apparent chaos was in fact under control, and everything was working evenly towards the clearance.

Mr. Carnegie, assisted by Mr. E. J. Rowe and Mr. Criswell, his assistant County Surveyors, set themselves to their tasks, which they divided into four phases:—(i) The recovery of the living and dead in Lynmouth and flood area; (ii) An immediate reconnaissance of the damage to Lynmouth and the whole flood area; (iii) The Temporary phase of reconstruction and (iv) The final complete and permanent phase of reconstruction.

With the large number of personnel necessary, the Royal Castle Hotel, Lynton, was taken over as temporary headquarters, and accommodation was also given to the Army Technicians. It was here that a very young Lance-Corporal, R.E., who had been loaned to the County, took over the telephone switchboard, and though quite inexperienced carried on to such good effect that in the speed and pressure of events he was quite forgotten. When they did think of him forty-eight hours later, he was still on the job and uncomplaining.

During the night of the disaster there was not a single casualty calling for first aid treatment, but when the clearance work commenced, a steady stream of minor casualties had to be dealt with. For this purpose the local St. John Ambulance Brigade set up a first aid post at the foot of Lynmouth Hill, and it was kept busy for the next four weeks. Altogether well over three hundred minor casualties were treated. A number of major casualties occurred in the later stages of the reconstruction work.

So far in these pages, an attempt has been made to retain some semblance of continuity in narrating the sequence of events. On Monday, the 18th, however, when the full weight of the magnificent organisation began to dovetail as a coherent whole, the various facets of the scene became merged, as indeed did the days and nights, and it is only possible to try and give an overall picture of the fine work that went on. More detailed description of the work of the many organisations and societies appears in the pages which follow.

It was known that at least thirty and possibly as many as sixty people were missing, and the grim work of searching for the bodies of victims was in itself a major operation. In the town the search was continued by police and men of the fire service. In the swollen estuary military frogmen carried out investigations. This part of the work also had the assistance of an R.A.F. launch with a policeman who was equipped with a Walkie-Talkie apparatus on board. Motor-boats too were searching along the coast and Inspector Wheeler and Constable Harper, aided by commandos went down the otherwise inaccessible seven-hundred-foot cliff on the end of a rope to see if they could discover anything at the foot of the rocks.

The task upon which the County Surveyor and his men concentrated was in clearing the havoc below Prospect Corner, and redirecting the West Lyn to its original course. "Clearing" is an understatement, for the work entailed removal of many thousand of tons of silt and rubble, and the dynamiting of the massive boulders which were strewn about everywhere, to get them to a size convenient to handle. Military forces were drafted in to assist in this work.

The whole area had been cordoned off by the Police, who had established six control posts including that at Blackmoor Gate (seven miles from Lynmouth). The Somerset Police also established posts on their side.

The national interest and sympathy in the whole tragedy was reflected by the fact that some fifty representatives of the Press were in the immediate vicinity. B.B.C. Television teams, news reel reporters and photographers were always about the scene, recording and reporting every item of interest in order that the outside world could be kept posted with the up-to-date developments. The photographer from *Life*, the American magazine, flew over specially one day, took his pictures and flew back to America a few days later.

Passes issued by the Town Clerk in the Town Hall had been given to the residents, to enable them to get through to their houses and premises in order to search for valuables and property. Eventually, however, it was found that the civilians were seriously impeding progress, and somewhat courageously —for it was an unpopular though very necessary action—the

Chief Constable gave authority for a complete closing of Lynmouth, except to those actually employed on the work of reconstruction.

Sunday had been a day of patchwork repairs and clearance, for much heavier equipment was necessary in phase one, than was available in the vicinity. In far off places, the wheels began to turn, and the new week commenced the greatest combined operation ever seen in Britain in times of peace came into being. Never had there been a greater concentration of heavy plant in so small an area.

There were hundreds of County Council employees working in gangs, contractors' men and their lorries drawn from all over Devon and parts of Somerset; police from all over the county, men drawn from a score or more different units of the Regular Army, including frogmen; Territorials from their camp in Cornwall; personnel from the Royal Air Force, Fire Service, Civil Defence, Women's Voluntary Services, St. John Ambulance and British Red Cross, R.S.P.C.A. Inspectors, Salvation Army and N.A.A.F.I.—all were represented and working as a team.

Every possible scientific aid that might serve a purpose was brought in. The Police obtained and operated Walkie-Talkie (short wave wireless sets); there were motor-cycle despatch riders and mobile public address equipment. The Army supplied searchlights, their own engineering workshops, laundry and bath units.

There were the National bodies. The Ministry of Food sent a mobile canteen, the Assistance Board a travelling office for the issue of travelling warrants and cash grants for those who were destitute. A Ministry of Labour mobile unit arrived for the registry of unemployed and the payments of benefits.

There were personnel and equipment of the Electricity undertaking, the Water Board and Post Office Telephone Engineers. The R.A.C. and A.A. organisations helped in traffic control and the general aid to motorists. There were squads of townspeople assisting in salvage work, whilst others were manning Rest Centres and the Information Bureau.

Above all, the "Heavies" began to arrive. Without specialised equipment, the whole village would have had to be written off as a complete loss. So, from Carlisle and Darlington in the North, from Salisbury and London in the South, wherever the Army depots lay, the "giants" began to move. Massive bulldozers, excavators, Scammel loaders, travelling generating stations, emergency water tenders, cranes and a variety of other vehicles of all types began to lumber towards the stricken village. Travelling night and day, setting traffic problems to local Police Forces in a dozen areas on their journey, they came to Lynmouth. On the bulldozer blades or on the sides of the vehicles were chalked slogans—"Operation Flood", "Lynmouth Lil" and "Lynmouth here we come". Men, women and children cheered them on their way, as they passed through towns, villages and hamlets. Tea and buns were lavished on the men, and it is certain that many an ex-serviceman of the last world war watched and felt a little out of it all.

On arrival, completely new sets of problems presented themselves to the harassed men in charge, who were already combating, by ingenious means, the difficult terrain of North Devon. The only access to Lynmouth was by way of Lynmouth Hill, with its severe hair pin bends and gradient of one-in-four. Furthermore, the road was but a mere shelf cut in the rocky gorge. These mechanical monsters weighed, together with their equipment, some *fifty tons*, and it was necessary to have two other Scammel recovery vehicles preceding them and another hooked on behind which, when they were in low gear, proved an effective brake. In the early stages this was done at night to avoid interference with the other traffic. So these enormous convoys with a hissing of air brakes and the screech of mechanical brakes, went down the hill at a snail's pace blocking the road and all other traffic for an hour at a time.

"The Scammels are coming" became a catch-phrase with Military Police, when the word went round that traffic was to stop to enable another convoy to descend the hill. Most of the M.P.'s were Scotsmen. They spoke the broad Doric of their country, and one could discern the pride with which they linked the phrase with that of the famous Clan Campbell of long ago.

At one point of the operations, cracks were discovered in the road at a time when a good deal of Army transport was going up and down, and the Chief Constable assumed the responsibility of stopping all traffic until the County Surveyor had again inspected the road and supporting embankment. It was most unfortunate that the hold-up occurred when a highly placed officer was visiting the scene and the troops had to be at a standstill, but no undue risk dared be taken with the only road into the heart of the operations.

Once a pathway had been cleared through the debris at Prospect Corner, a dozen or more bulldozers went into action in the river itself with the purpose of establishing a normal channel and getting it back to its usual depth, for the river bed was some *six feet higher* than pre-flood. Working down from Lyndale Bridge to the estuary, those Army vehicles did yeoman service. Operated for the most part by young fellows who were "Z" Reservists, the "dozers" were made to execute the most amazing evolutions. They pushed silt and boulders before them and then slowly but inexorably up an incline, to form a barrier against further inroads by the sea. The incredible angles at which the caterpillars could maintain balance, had to be seen to be believed. The operators vied with each other to coax their machines to excavate or push more material than the man operating the same machine on the last shift. They averaged a thousand tons a shift.

From time to time a vehicle gave up before the strain and broke down midstream, marooning the operator in the middle of a small sea. Another vehicle would then set off to the rescue, carrying an engineer who would jump from one vehicle to the other, make temporary repairs and so allow the disabled member to reach the river bank again.

When it was found that girders of a certain length were required for bridging and that they were not available in the area, enquiries went out all over the country, and at last British Railways saved the situation by finding some of suitable length in their store and sending them down by special lorry. It was typical of the co-operation received everywhere.

Tractors puffed and churned as they wrenched at large trees which had been deposited on the beach, in order to get them clear. Power saws with their high pitched note slashed through the heavy tree trunks. The incessant noise made by these monsters added to the general din of excavators, other bulldozers, the ringing of pneumatic drills, the detonating of dynamite charges used to break down the boulders. The noise was deafening as it filled the valley and in a fruitless effort to escape, reverberated round and round the hills which rose from five hundred to a thousand feet on three sides.

The work was severe on vehicles, but it must have been a gruelling task for the operators. The continuous jolting and shaking over boulders, added to the noise of the engine for eight and a half hours at a time, was no joy ride. Operation "Estuary" and Operation "King Canute" were in full swing.

Altogether 100,000 tons of boulders and silt were bulldozed from the river, 40,000 tons of which went to building up the sea-wall as a protection against the sea. A further 100,000 tons was cleared from the shattered town itself.

At this time the operations gave every impression of a war time scene, with some of the troops doing their washing and hanging it up to dry.

All over the village, parties of men were working. Fire Service personnel were clearing cellars of debris, then pumping them free of foul water, salvaging goods and destroying perishable stores, boarding up windows, and a hundred and one other tasks. Above all, they were contributing perhaps the greatest of all blessings—the lavish distribution of strong disinfectant which gradually mastered the dank smell of flood water and the awful stench of sewage which had remained like a pall over everything since the pipe system was smashed and rendered useless by the flood.

The supplying of fresh water was, of course, a problem which had to be met in the very early stages. It had been discovered, however, that the filters at the waterworks had suffered no serious damage, although the water had become polluted. A warning was issued by Dr. Nightingale, Medical Officer, that it was dangerous even to brush the teeth without first boiling the water. On Sunday, Military and R.A.F. vehicles together with those of the North Devon Water Board brought in, by tanker, supplies which were dispensed from the Town Hall. Typical of the spirit was the slogan chalked on an R.A.F. tanker, from which supplies were being issued:—"Same old firm—Business as Usual." It was indeed the same old firm—the men of the armed forces, whose cheerful spirit and kindness of heart was a great help to those they were serving. A lorry sent by Messrs. Horlicks from Ilminster, contained seven hundred gallons of water in milk churns. It was amazing that the driver of this vehicle was able to accomplish the very difficult journey through greatly flooded areas.

Meanwhile considerable concern was felt over the defence-less state of what buildings remained, if further heavy rain coincided with a high tide. Another section of the Army was put to work making an embankment of sand bags. Out in the estuary, Army frogmen were concentrating on reconnoitring for the one hundred and thirty missing vehicles, which might contain the bodies of their owners. When the cars were discovered it often proved a herculean task to get them ashore, for in most cases they were filled with stones and debris and were a dead-weight. One by one they were collected. What were beautiful sleek models a day or two before were now elongated or square masses of rusted metal. Some of them looked as if they had suffered a giant squeeze. All the component parts were there, but had been compressed to a quarter of the length and height. If more evidence was needed of the enormous forces unleashed by nature, it was evident in the wrecks of those cars. Strange to say however, the tyres had proved their resilience and very few were even flat.

With the aid of the Army searchlights and the scores of 1000 and 1500 watt lamps loaned and fitted by the Electricity Authority, the work went on day and night; and gradually at first, then with increasing speed, chaos began to give way to order.

It was early on Sunday that a plank foot-bridge was thrown across the West Lyn, so that contact could be renewed with the Somerset side. On the same day Army officers began to survey the position at Barbrook with a view to erecting a Bailey bridge at that point. Very soon two hundred Royal Engineers of the 121 Army Engineers (T.A.) who had detrained for camp at Penhale, near Newquay, but had immediately volunteered for relief duty, commenced the operation. They worked to such effect that on Saturday, August 23rd., at 3. 15 a.m. the old bridge of twenty foot span was replaced by a ninety foot span Bailey bridge, the latter constructed overnight. Progress was good and everyone was pleased. No wonder there were drinks all round with a bottle of rum added to the beer to give it body.

Later, the Army built a Bailey bridge with a span of seventy feet on concrete abutments, to replace the old Hillsford bridge. This was a particularly difficult clearing operation, including felling of trees some of which were twenty-four inch diameter. The bridge was completed and at midnight was officially opened by Major General C. L. Firbank, C.B.E., D.S.O., Commanding South West District. A typical Army touch was the planting of flowers in the approaches to their finished work.

The age of miracles was not passed. Within five days the County Surveyor was able to announce the completion of the first stage emergency work. Communication with the Countisbury side had been restored, the sea wall had been temporarily repaired, many bridges replaced and there was a feeling of hope abroad again.

Altogether some 121 motor vehicles were salvaged from the area. Of this number twenty-eight were totally wrecked and twenty-four extensively damaged. In addition, a further thirty-eight vehicles were reported to have been in the district but no trace of them has ever been found. By arrangement the R.A.C. and the A.A. undertook the identification of these vehicles.

The number of boats lost totalled nineteen.

As more and more equipment and personnel came to Lynton, the car park took the form of field headquarters. Part of the Repair Shops of the Royal Engineers and R.E.M.E. were situated there (a forward element operated from the river bank in Lynmouth), and were kept fully employed. The very difficult nature of the work put a severe strain on Army plant, and twenty-five per cent needed repairs after every shift. In addition, over a hundred Army vehicles engaged in first aid work on Exmoor were maintained by these workshops, and assistance was given to the County in the maintenance of their plant. Altogether 198 plant and vehicle repair jobs were completed by R.E.M.E., quite apart from vehicle recovery tasks.

When the very difficult country and conditions are taken into account, it is amazing that the whole episode passed off with so few accidents, a fact which reflects the highest credit on the extraordinary skill of the personnel—military and civilian—who were engaged on the work.

If emphasis on the difficulties of the country is required it is only necessary to consider the following hills—by no means an exhaustive list—which immediately surround Lynton and Lynmouth:-

Lynmouth Hill	700	yards	Gradient	1 in 4.
Countisbury	2000	,,	,,	1 in 4.
Parracombe	700	,,	,,	1 in 6.
Beggar's Roost	500	,,	,,	1 in 4.
Dean Steep	500	,,	,,	1 in 5.
Kitscombe	600	,,	,,	1 in 4.
Mannacott	800	,,	,,	1 in 4.

One accident occurred when a ten-ton Army tractor, towing a sixteen-wheel twenty-ton trailer, left the road on Lynmouth Hill at a point where there was a precipitous drop of several hundred feet. An Army recovery team was sent to the spot and worked to secure and save the two vehicles. For two hours a comparatively small tree in the side of the gorge took the strain of the trailer, but the position was considered to be so hopeless that the officer in charge of the recovery received permission to abandon the trailer if absolutely necessary. After two hours the tree snapped, but by that time the trailer had been secured by wire hawsers and it was safe. For twenty-one hours, non-stop, the recovery team slaved at the job, using huge Scammel vehicles, oxy-acetylene equipment, etc. in their efforts. After the road had been closed for thirty-six hours, their efforts were crowned with success. It was certainly a notable achievement.

A further accident, in which by a miracle no one was hurt, occurred when a three-ton petrol tanker from Yeovil, driven by a lance corporal of the R.A.S.C., got out of control down Countisbury Hill. The tanker crashed into Lyndale bridge and farther on into the temporary wooden bridge. Fortunately strong wooden piles prevented the tanker from falling into the river. The driver kept his nerve, and sounding his horn continuously, scattered pedestrians. A policeman, sitting on the bridge with his back to the lorry, had the fright of his life when the tanker careered by and grazed his knee. He had not heard its approach, nor the consternation around him, due to the listening equipment he had on his head.

Another three-ton Army truck conveying a working party left the road at a hair pin bend and overturned down the wooded hillside. There were twenty passengers, and one Officer and six other ranks were injured.

*   *   *

Perhaps as heartening to the people as anything else was the concern and interest displayed in their trouble by Her Majesty's Ministers and other important personages.

A day or two after the disaster, the Rt. Hon. Harold Macmillan, Minister of Housing and Local Government, visited the scene of devastation, and said that the sight of Lynmouth reminded him of Ypres in the First World war. He was appalled by what he had seen, and promised that the Ministries concerned would co-operate in the task of restoration and would ultimately decide the various financial responsibilities. He then attended a meeting of representative bodies at the Town Hall, at which the decision was confirmed that Mr. Carnegie should be made Controller of all reconstruction work.

No time was lost. Next morning Mr Macmillan reported to the Cabinet on his visit and consequently the Ministries of Transport, Health, Works, Labour and Agriculture and Fisheries, in addition to his own Ministry, were brought into the scheme of relief. Furthermore, the Government immediately made a donation of £25,000 to the Relief Fund, and promised grants in aid of the rebuilding up to one hundred per cent.

The Rt. Hon. A. T. Lennox-Boyd, M.P., Minister of Transport and Civil Aviation, also visited the site by helicopter, accompanied by his Chief Administrative and Enquiry Officials. The purpose of his visit was to inspect the engineering works on roads and bridges and to discuss, with local officials, the works in which his Ministry would be involved both in the emergency and permanent phases of reconstruction.

Mr. Lennox-Boyd made a detailed tour of the operations and after discussion with Colonel T. Gracey, Chairman of Devon Roads Committee and Chairman of the Devon River Board, he addressed the Council and Officials, expressing his approval of the manner in which the clearing up operations were being conducted, and his thanks for the great help being given by the Army.

It is interesting to note that this was the first occasion on which a Transport Minister of Her Majesty's Government had flown by helicopter from London, to the scenes of operations administered by his Ministry.

After the first week, a tremendous change had been effected. The achievement of results was summed up by the headings in a national Sunday Newspaper:—

A SUNNY SUNDAY
HERE IS NEWS TO WARM YOUR HEART.
LYNMOUTH—NO RED TAPE, NO FUSS, NO DELAY
SWIFT DECISIVE ACTION

Later, other important visitors who went to see for themselves included:—Mr. W. C. Johnson, H.M. Inspector of Constabulary; Sir John Lienhop, Agent General for Victoria, Australia, and the Chief Constable of Somerset.

*   *   *

Under the energetic chairmanship of Mr. E. J. Pedder, Lynton's Council Housing Committee did not delay in facing up to the enormous problem created by the homeless, and arising from conversations between the Chairman and Lady Eldon the idea of the Caravan Park, as a temporary measure, grew. Lady Eldon, with her accustomed energy, lost no time in putting the idea into practice and an instant nation-wide appeal for one hundred caravans was issued. Immediately offers poured in from far and near, and several outright gifts of caravans were made. The first came from Mrs. Green of Seagree village near Chippenham, who presented a caravan outright to the Red Cross and all its contents to the occupants. At the end of two weeks the Holman Camp of some thirty caravans was ready for occupation. In all fifty-five caravans were arranged—the bulk in Holman Park, three were sent to Brendon and two to Barnstaple for special cases.

The moving and arranging of the homes on wheels was undertaken by the Caravan Society of Great Britain. Quantities of goods and chattels were collected and a large store opened in Lynton, with drawing power on much bigger stocks at the Red Cross Headquarters at Taunton and clothing stores at Heathfield Camp. All caravans were fully equipped with seventy-two items of domestic furnishings, which were presented as a gift to the occupants.

These temporary homes gradually emptied as permanent housing was found for the occupants. Some thirteen caravans remained in use at the beginning of 1953, but by the end of March the camp had closed down and caravans were returned to their owners, except six which had been presented outright. A camp warden was on permanent duty at the Park during its occupation.

Help was offered from a variety of sources. An essential need was supplied by the Hotpoint Electrical Appliance Co. Ltd., who set up a communal laundry which was a blessing not only to the forty-eight families in the Caravan Park but a similar number of evacuees who were in billets. The laundry was fully equipped with every electrical appliance to delight the housewife's heart. There were washing machines, wringers, ironers, steel sink units and even pegs. Demonstrators spent a week on the site, teaching the use of the equipment.

The initial emergency was being covered by the Caravan Park, but practical measures were immediately put in hand for permanent dwellings. As early as September 8th, a start was made on some bungalows, and four weeks later eight Cornish Unit bungalows were ready to receive the first tenants. Close by, further three-bedroom units were commenced shortly afterwards, until preparation had been made for a total of thirty. They were situated on a new road—Hume Avenue.

H.R.H. the Duke of Edinburgh paid a visit to West Somerset, Exmoor, Lynton and Lynmouth in October 1952, to see for himself the damage that had been caused by the floods. He made a tour of Lynmouth and had the position explained to him by Mrs. D. Slater (Chairman of the Council). He was accompanied by Lord and Lady Fortescue, Sir John Shelley (Chairman of the Devon County Council), Mr. R. B. Carnegie and other officials.

The ascent to Lynton from Lynmouth was accomplished by the Cliff Railway, and His Royal Highness was the first Royal passenger ever carried in the sixty-two years of the railway's existence. The party visited the Holman Caravan Park, which His Royal Highness thought was a marvellous temporary solution to the housing problem which had to be faced as a result of the disaster.

The first of the eight new bungalows was opened by the Duke of Edinburgh with a silver key, which bore the inscription —"Lynmouth Flood Disaster 1952. First completed house for the homeless opened by H.R.H. the Duke of Edinburgh, K.G." The key was afterwards handed to Mrs. Slater, who had it framed and it now hangs in the bungalow, No. 1, Hume Avenue. The Duke inspected the house after the official opening.

Congratulating an eighty-one-year-old gentleman temporarily housed in a caravan, the Duke asked whether he would be glad to be going back to his home. "Yes," replied the veteran, "this is a bit too close to the cemetery for my liking!" (The cemetery was two fields away).

To further assist the housing, Messrs. R. Costain Ltd., Civil Engineering Contractors, London, presented two houses costing £2,000 each to the Urban District Council.

THE FLOODS IN THE WIDER AREA

Whilst the purpose of this book is to cover the story of the floods as far as the main focal point—Lynmouth—is concerned, some mention, however brief, must be made of the other isolated spots where the flood waters caused disaster as overwhelming in their ferocity as occurred in the town of Lynmouth, although nowhere was it so concentrated.

Everywhere there was at least one common peril—the suddenness of the disaster. Four miles up the valley of the river Heddon, a veritable lake of water was trapped through the blocking of the culverts in a fifty foot embankment. When at last the volume of the water caused the banks to burst, a huge wave descended on to the little village of Parracombe, three-quarters of a mile away. The terrified inhabitants heard the roar of the approaching torrent as they waited, already knee-deep in water, behind bolted doors.

The flooding of Parracombe started at about 9.30 p.m., when the Heddon rose over the little stone bridge in the centre of the village and entered most of the lower cottages, the smithy, half-a-dozen garages and the Fox and Goose Inn. Customers at the hotel crowded on top of the bar and others ran upstairs as the water entered the lower rooms and rose rapidly. It rushed over the bar counter and put out the kitchen stove before subsiding. Most of the customers then went home thinking the storm had abated.

Then about 12.45 a.m. there was a roar of racing waters, which struck the village bridge with the force of a bomb, scattering the twelve inch stone parapet in the middle of the street, ripping off patches of three-inch macadam surface from the road, and storming across to the hotel. The water broke in the downstairs windows and doors and rushed through to the back, sweeping trees into the rooms. The back door burst open and the torrent went on its way through the hotel garden.

Mr. A. Smyth and his wife, of Bridge House, heard the bridge collapse just as they were re-entering their kitchen from the back of the house. The front door and kitchen door seemed to be forced open simultaneously, and the flood water rushed into the room. Before Mr. and Mrs. Smyth could escape, the back door flew open and another torrent streamed in. The currents met at the kitchen door, trapping Mrs. Smyth between the door and the jamb. Waist-deep in water, Mr. Smyth released his wife and helped her upstairs.

It is believed that Mr. W. J. Leaworthy, aged sixty, went out twice that night to help others. The first time he had been to assist his sister in saving her furniture. Two hours later, he waded out into the darkness to see if she was all right. He never came back, and his body was found a mile downstream among a mass of debris.

In a holiday chalet at Mill Farm, a visitor from Surrey, Mrs. A. Thorne, and her fourteen-year-old son were presumably asleep when the water swept the chalet and its occupants away into the darkness. Their bodies were subsequently discovered a mile away.

At New Mill Farm, which lies between Lynton and Parracombe, a normally small tributary and the West Lyn river merge. In their greatly swollen state they deviated from their usual channel and swept towards the farmhouse. Fortunately, a six ton hayrick stood in the path of the waters. It was picked up and swept along as if it was of no weight at all and thrown against the farmhouse, in which position it acted as a buttress and undoubtedly saved the building.

Much damage was caused at Challacombe, when the river Bray flooded. The road was washed away for a three-mile length and badly rutted to a depth, in some places, of four feet. There was flooding at Brayford, Winsford and other isolated hamlets and villages.

In the early hours of Saturday morning, a baby boy was born at a marooned farm at Brendon. The mother was on a visit to the farm and was unable to leave owing to the cloudburst. Not until four hours after the birth were neighbours able to lay stepping stones to the farm to enable ambulance men to cross where the road had been torn away. They then evacuated the mother and child by ambulance.

At Brendon also parts of the bungalow occupied by Mr. Lang were swept away, as was also a special barrel of beer which Mr. Lang had brewed and was storing until it was tapped in celebration of his seventieth birthday. Mr. Lang's barrel was never found, but a firm of brewers, hearing of the incident, made good his loss.

At Simonsbath, the village in the heart of Exmoor which is always the first to be isolated when snow falls, a small tributary of the river Barle became a torrent and rose suddenly about ten to twelve feet above normal, flooding houses in the vicinity. It happened so quickly that sixty-eight-year-old Frank Vigars, who was in the backyard of his premises, had to enter his house and rescue his wife and two grand-daughters, who were floating about in the kitchen. He carried them to safety on his back. A nearby hotel, which stands on another tributary of the Barle, was flooded to ceiling height.

Another tragedy occurred at Shallowford, Filleigh, which resulted in three Manchester Boy Scouts losing their lives. The troop of Scouts was camping in the meadows, and in the early hours of Saturday morning when the waters rose suddenly, the lads woke to find the camp completely awash. Most of them struggled to safety and upon reaching higher ground the Scout-master made a quick check and found that four boys were missing. He immediately went back and found one of them clinging to the branches of a tree after having been washed fifty yards down-stream. Although a search was made, the three other boys could not be found. Their bodies were recovered later. The troop which numbered twenty-one, lost every bit of their equipment and clothes.

When the news of the disaster reached South Molton, an appeal was at once launched by the Mayor to replace the boys' equipment, valued at between £300/400. Every house in the Borough was canvassed by volunteers and Scouts and there were special collections in the churches and cinemas.

The village of Dulverton in Somerset also suffered severely, and but for swift action and advance warning—short though it was—by the Police, there might have been a serious loss of life.

In the early hours of the morning the river Barle overflowed its banks and flooded the lower parts of the town. Uprooted trees acted as battering rams and destroyed buildings indiscriminately. When the bridge became blocked, the water swept away each side of the structure and with it went part of a house: the three families had just time to escape through a hole in the roof. A little farther on, a garage and two cars were washed away, and a larger garage containing twelve vehicles received the full impact of the water. All the vehicles were carried into the river. All roads to the village were quite impassable for a day or two, and four fire engines were despatched from Taunton to assist in pumping and clearance work.

At Exford, which lies on the river Exe and in the middle of the hunting country, havoc was caused. Beside the White Horse Hotel, twenty-two horses were stabled. When the river rose, part of the stables was swept away and the water rose to eight feet. The frightened beasts were liberated by a groom and huntsman and made their way from the approaching wall of water, only to find that they were running into it in the other direction. The leading animal then turned again and made away to higher ground, all the others following him. Next day all but two of the horses were found. The errant two were rounded up on the moor a few days later.

Mr. D. Rolfe, proprietor of the White Horse, said that in a matter of minutes the water rose over the whole of the ground floor of the hotel to a height of five feet. The position was not helped by the fact that several tons of manure and forage oats piled beyond the stables were carried down to the building by the onrush of water which tore off doors and windows and even carried along a new car, toppling the vehicle over and over until it reached the bridge.

When the water subsided there was an amazing tribute to British craftsmanship. A Lister diesel engine in one of the stables was covered by six feet of water *yet* it had continued to work all night. Thus Exford, which was connected to the hotel's electrical eqipment in case of emergency, had light throughout its night of horror.

When the door of a toilet in the hotel was opened next morning, a large eel was found imprisoned there. It was accompanied by a huge toad, which was only discernible by its two bright eyes.

*   *   *

The Army's operation "Elkforce" carried out the reconnaissance and work of repair in the outlying places on Exmoor. Altogether twenty-five officers and at times as many as thirteen hundred other ranks were on these projects. The number of Army vehicles rose from fifty-four to ninety-five, in addition to twenty-seven jeeps, which were found invaluable for investigation work over rough country.

Over one hundred and fourteen operations were carried out for farmers. The work included the repair or erection of walls, fences, temporary bridges, roads, diversion of streams and river clearance. No task was too small, none too large. Co-operation between all concerned was so close that as one Army "wag" put it:—"At Dulverton, Army and Police even shared a loose box as headquarters."

The work was particularly hard on the officers, who carried out reconnaissance all day and then went into conference to plan the next day's operations. Often it meant a fourteen to sixteen hour day with work from dawn to dusk, regardless of weather conditions.

Whilst the emphasis in this chapter has been on the Army's operation "Elkforce", a tremendous amount of work in the outlying districts in the County area was carried out by the Devon County Council staff, in which some two hundred workmen were engaged. The administrative personnel included:—

R. B. Carnegie, C.B.E. (County Surveyor).

H. Criswell, B.SC. (Assistant County Surveyor).

E. J. Rowe (Assistant County Surveyor).

R. J. Ayres (Area Surveyor).

K. G. Whalley, G. A. Stedman and S. T. Ford (Divisional Surveyors).

E. P. Dyer (Administrative Officer).

Engineering Assistants and Draughtsmen, Accounts and Correspondence Clerks, Typists, etc., who were temporarily at the Royal Castle Hotel as Headquarters.

SOMBRE SCENES

THE INQUEST.

A pathetic note was struck when the Inquest was held on the first victims. The little dog of Councillor Tom Floyd, who had been through the same ordeal as his master, just hated to be parted from him and he whimpered at the door outside the premises as if pleading not to be separated again. It was a human touch of the Coroner to give instructions for Tim to be admitted. He joined his master and sat silently through the proceedings, adding pathos to an already tragic scene.

The Coroner returned a verdict of "Accidental death due to storm and flood."

*　　　*　　　*

THE FUNERAL.

The funeral of the first thirteen victims of the flood took place on Friday, August 22nd, in the Lynton cemetery.

It was a bright, warm and sunny afternoon, and the slow winding procession gave rise to a tumult of emotions in all who watched or took part. The procession was one of sombre colours. The blue jerseys of the fishermen, the Council and County officials in deep mourning and variegated uniforms of police, firemen, W.V.S., Salvation Army, Red Cross, St. John Ambulance and men of the regular Services in khaki and air force blue. All who had gone to help the stricken people mixed with those who had lived through the disaster, and were present to mourn and pay a last tribute to their relatives, friends and neighbours whose coffins they were following.

Acting as bearers were men of the Fire Service.

No more peaceful setting than the lovely little cemetery nestling beneath the hills at the entrance of the Valley of Rocks, could be imagined. Within the sound but out of sight of the sea, the rugged grandeur of the rock projections, the colouring of the hills on the far side of the valley, all combined to make a perfect setting for so touching an occasion.

The bowed heads, the steady, unfaltering and comforting tones of the clergy, the sobbing of the relatives and the low murmur from all present as the service came to a close, made a deep impression.

As the last rites were completed, the strains of the bagpipes played by a piper of the 4/5th Scots Fusiliers, broke the deep silence. The mournful and pathetic notes of *Land of the Leal* and *Flowers of the Forest* echoed through the hills, and in a country that is so typical of parts of Scotland, it seemed to be a tribute that somehow fitted the solemn occasion.

No more fitting description of the valley and the hillside will ever be written, than that by Southey:—

"But all the middle of the valley was a place to rest in, to sit and think that troubles were not if we would not make them. To know the sea outside the hill, but never to behold it".

NOTE: Months afterwards it was learned that the grave of the unknown woman, buried apart from the other flood victims, had received special attention and was planted with bulbs from the attendant's own garden. He did not like to feel "that the poor lady was neglected." A touching reminder of the sympathy that was at all times evident throughout the disaster.

In Memoriam

Name	Age	Address
ADA BARWICK	60	Lynmouth
ELSIE D. BOWEN	32	Lynton
RONALD BOWEN	37	Lynton
KENNETH R. F. BOWEN	9	Lynton
DERRICK BREDDY	11	Manchester
ELSIE CHERRY	56	Highgate, London
BENJAMIN COULT	56	Durham
EMMA COULT	52	Durham
RODNEY G. DIMMOCK	8	Lynton
MARY A. FLOYD	64	Lynton
FREDERICK C. FLOYD	27	Lynton
JOYCE HISCOCK	21	Australian on holiday
HANNAH JARVIS	77	Lynmouth
WILLIAM J. LEAWORTHY	60	Parracombe
GABRIEL J. LITSON	78	Lynmouth
CHARLES H. LITSON	53	Lynmouth
GWENDA OXLEY	22	Australian on holiday
WILLIAM N. RICHARDS	30	Lynmouth
GWENDOLINE A. RICHARDS	32	Lynmouth
BERNARD G. RICHARDS	3	Lynmouth
ERNEST W. RICHARDS	3 months	Lynmouth
EMILY RIDD	54	Lynton
GEOFFREY ROBINSON	11	Manchester
HAROLD SHAW	14	Manchester
EDWIN SMITH	50	Lynmouth
ALYS THORNE	46	Woking, Surrey
ROGER THORNE	14	Woking, Surrey
MAUD E. WATTS	72	Lynmouth
WILLIAM H. WATTS	80	Lynmouth

One lady unidentified.

MISSING AND BELIEVED DROWNED

Name	Age	Address
STELLA BATES	40	Lynmouth
DAVID T. BOWEN	11	Lynton
ELIZABETH CANNON	75	Lynmouth
JESSIE WHITBREAD	48	Lynmouth

THE MEMORIAL SERVICE.

Exactly two weeks after the disaster a Memorial Service was held in the fine old Parish Church of St. Mary the Virgin at Lynton. It was broadcast to the nation by the B.B.C.

Long before the service began, residents of the area entered the church to await the arrival from Lynton Town Hall of a procession headed by the Earl Fortescue, Lord Lieutenant of the County, who represented Her Majesty the Queen. The procession was led by a detachment of the Devon Constabulary, who formed a Guard of Honour at the gates of the Church.

In a moving address the Bishop of Exeter, Dr. R. C. Mortimer, said it was a strange and bitter irony indeed, that the very things which constituted the charm of Lynmouth—the trees, the rocks and boulders over which the streams leapt and foamed and the very streams themselves—had turned into the engines and instruments of destruction.

He suggested that when it was all over, a plain cross should be erected where the waters broke through (opposite Lyndale Hotel)—a plain cross as a sign of our freedom from the fear of death and a sign of our real and true security, in spite of our seeming insecurity. A cross, he added, is a sign not simply of death but of death followed by resurrection.

The service was conducted by the vicar of Lynton, the Rev. E. H. Souttar, assisted by the Vicar of Lynmouth, the Rev. A. T. Coldman and the Congregational Minister the Rev. J. Potts.

Simultaneously, at the request of workmen on the site, the Salvation Army held a brief Memorial Service in Lynmouth. It was a strange and moving sight to see two hundred begrimed soldiers and workmen drop their tools when the wail of a hand-cranked siren sounded as a signal that the service was about to commence. Perched on bulldozers and lorries and standing round in a circle, the congregation listened intently as Mrs. Brigadier Holland of the South West Divisional Headquarters, Plymouth, read the forty-sixth Psalm.

During the fortnight of temporary reconstruction, it was the only time that complete silence had reigned. For the brief fifteen minutes, the roar of bulldozers, excavators, lorries and compressors was stilled while the service was conducted in memory of those who had lost their lives.

THE WORLD SHOWS PRACTICAL SYMPATHY

When Lynmouth's plight became known to the country and the world, the flood-gates of generosity were opened. The W.V.S. National Appeal for clothing brought an instant response, and within a few days it was absolutely impossible to handle the vast quantities of parcels that began to descend on Lynton. The County W.V.S. organisation, therefore, made available a packing and sorting depot at Heathfield, near Newton Abbot. This depot was daily staffed by one hundred and twenty voluntary workers who received, opened and sorted more than 12,000 parcels in six weeks. Many contained gifts of food as well as clothing, and for this reason when the need had long passed, every parcel had to be opened with as little delay as possible. Parcels also contained gifts of money, ranging from cheques to a few pence. The money was acknowledged and passed to the Lord Lieutenant's Relief Fund. Although most of the parcels were sent anonymously, there were some 21,500 letters of sympathy packed inside others. The British Railways and the Post Office announced that they would carry and deliver all parcels free of charge.

Four days was enough to strain every possible resource to the limit and the appeal went into reverse. A public announcement was made that no more parcels should be sent.

The wide ranges of other gifts sent to Lynton Town Hall varied from complete houses and caravans down to carpet cleaning soap, and the quantities of most of the items were staggering. They included:—

A truck load of slates from the Welsh quarries

Paints for house decoration

A consignment of disinfectant

Fireplaces and electric fires

House furnishing and linen

Sports gear for a youth club

Toys and sweets

Ladies' handbags and necklaces

Pressure lamps

Oil paintings of Lynmouth

Equipment for caravans

Furnishings for caravans and houses

Cutlery and crockery

Toys came by air from America, cases of tinned food from New Zealand and even the Englishman's love of gardening was not lost sight of, for currant bushes and raspberry canes, daffodil, tulip and iris bulbs and even strawberry plants were sent to Lynmouth from various parts of the country in large quantities.

Perhaps one of the most pathetic aspects of these gifts was the number of wedding and engagement rings sent to help those in distress from, generally speaking, those who could ill afford anything else. One wedding ring was from a widow who had worn it for forty-five years of happily married life.

Mr. Ridge, the Town Clerk, became quite resigned to the fact that at any moment of the day he would be called from his office to find a pantechnicon outside with more gifts for Lynmouth.

In the early phases the County Surveyor was inundated by offers of help. The American Air Force offered to fly any item of plant required on the site. The Norwegian Chamber of Trade offered the loan of river technicians and staff. The Anglo-Iranian Oil Company offered engineering technicians, and Contractors from far and wide, machines and personnel. Two thousand gallons of disinfectant were sent by the National Coal Board. Suppliers of material were prepared to send tools, boots, protective clothing, soap. Anything and everything was available on request. Many County Councils, large and small Municipal Authorities and River Boards offered help in personnel and materials. Sandbags, timber, steel, plant, pumps—the list was never ending.

Sympathy flowed in from all parts of the world, and one of the highlights was the visit paid by Mr. W. A. Bustamante, the sixty-eight-year-old Chief Minister of the Jamaican Legislature. He came to express his personal sorrow and to reciprocate, if he could, the help which Great Britain had given to Jamaica when, twelve months before, their country was almost destroyed by a great hurricane.

The sympathy took a practical form, for he brought with him five tons of bananas, five tons of sugar and half-a-ton of coffee from Jamaica, as a gift to the residents of Lynmouth and the whole flood area.

Mr. Bustamante lived up to his world-wide reputation as a colourful and great personality. Tall with a powerful physique, his striking features, iron grey hair brushed straight up from his forehead, his cheerful disposition and deep ready laugh, made a great impression upon all with whom he came into contact.

At the Jubilee Hall, Lynton, he told the homeless that although in Jamaica they were five thousand miles away from Great Britain, he wanted them to feel that they were all part of the great British Empire and belonged to each other. When he spoke, he achieved a high standard of oratory and proved a

great success, particularly when he addressed the children.
Like many good speakers, he adopted a staccato style:—

*"Poor children, you shall long remember the terrible experience
through which you have passed. You shall have your lovely
homes rebuilt. You shall be happy. You shall forget. You
shall grow up lovely, strong people like your mummies and
daddies.*

*You shall have bananas. One ton, two ton, three ton, four
ton, five ton of bananas."*

During this part of his speech many "hands" of bananas
were handed round by his aides. Every women and child in the
vicinity were clutching bananas. Mr. Bustamante, to emphasize
the excellent taste and nutrition value of the banana, punctuated
his speech to the children by eating banana after banana:—

*"Banana good for Bustamante, banana good for children.
Make you big and strong like Bustamante. You people will
have coffee, half-a-ton of Jamaican coffee—five tons of
Jamaican sugar from the people of Jamaica."*

Later Mr. Bustamante was Guest of Honour at a dinner
given by the Ministry of Food which was held at the Valley of
Rocks Hotel. His visit will long be remembered in North Devon.

THE APPEAL

On Sunday, August 17th, 1952, a National Appeal was launched jointly by Earl Fortescue, the Lord Lieutenant of Devon and Lord Hylton, the Lord Lieutenant of Somerset. The Fund, opened under the title of *North Devon and West Somerset Relief Fund*, brought a response from all over the country, and indeed from all parts of the world, which was both immediate and staggering in its volume.

Inviting contributions from not only the people of the West Country but everyone who had known and loved Lynmouth, the Appeal went on:—

"... *This countryside that has given pleasure to so many will, we feel sure, be generously remembered in its hour of need by all those who have known it in happier days. We hope and believe that this fund will meet a generous response far beyond the confines of the West Country, for, in its romantic beauty and appeal, Lynmouth in particular was a possession, not of one county but of the nation.*"

On Sunday morning when the Appeal was launched, Mr. G. H. Hollis, manager of the National Provincial Bank, Exeter branch, was approached by Earl Fortescue to see if he would become treasurer. He consented and at that stage thought perhaps the Fund might reach £200,000.

When the bank opened on Monday morning, a member of the staff was deputed to look after the fund. Twenty-four hours, however, proved more than enough. In that time a special Post Office van delivered seven sacks of mail and went back for more.

It was a good start. In less time than it takes to tell, the help was supplemented until most of the thirty to forty staff in the building were involved. Every spare room had been utilized. The counters were heaped with mail which had to be opened, sorted and entered. The floor was ankle deep in used envelopes. Moreover, due to the Bank's regulations that all cash must be dealt with each night, the conditions quickly became overwhelming.

Customers volunteered to help in this gigantic task. Trestle tables were borrowed from the Cathedral, to make more counter space but still the mail arrived in vast quantities. The staff and voluntary helpers worked frantically, but it was 11.30 p.m. before they finished the daily total. On the following day, staff from other banks volunteered to help. They sent adding machines and other equipment. The County Council loaned an envelope opening machine. Duplicating machines were loaned but it was still as much as the workers could do to keep abreast of the work day by day.

Cheques, postal orders, treasury notes, postage stamps and, of course, cash poured in. Not only the coin of this realm but of countries all over the world. French and Belgian franc, American and Canadian dollars and even British saving stamps. The whole operation became so huge that it will ever remain the worst type of nightmare that a bank clerk need fear.

By the end of the first week other branches of the Bank in the area were sending relief staff to help. More space, more trestle tables, continuous re-arrangement of staff duties and on the Thursday, the fourth day of the appeal, seventeen and a half bags of mail and four hundred and eleven registered packets arrived and were dealt with.

A large number of envelopes contained letters of sympathy. One from two little girls included their photographs, to prove their *bona fide* as responsible collectors. Innkeepers and licensees all over the kingdom sent asking for permission to collect, and sent their ideas of appeal posters for their bars. Other letters contained offers of help in kind. Offers of hospitality for the homeless, caravans, prams, armchairs, the adoption of children, care of animals, temporary homes and a score of other forms of help were tendered. One letter from a little boy read:—"Mummy gave me some money for an ice cream, but I am sending it to you for the poor homeless people." Enclosed were two stamps value threepence. An older child enclosed the money given to her that morning for her school lunch. She had gone without. All the letters were wonderful in their expressions of sympathy.

But there was no end to the ramifications and complications. Jewellery, wedding and signet rings, dress rings, cigarette cases and even a pair of gold rimmed lorgnettes were sent in to be turned into money. A fur coat, some paintings and a farm tractor arrived to be auctioned for the Fund.

From every corner of Britain contributions were arriving. South Kesteven in Lincolnshire, the village of Painswick in the Cotswolds, Skipton in Yorkshire, Dunoon, Aberdeen and Ardrossan in Scotland, the four Newports—those in Monmouth, Isle of Wight, Pembroke and Salop—all sent their cheques. Money poured in from Machynlleth, Llanfairfechan, Llwchwr and Penrhyndeudraith. Remote Irish villages sent their contributions as did the City of Birmingham its £35,000. The British Government sent £25,000. But these were from the British Isles —one could understand this expression of sympathy.

By now, however, the Lynmouth disaster was world news and so a second rush started. Money arrived from Penang, Zanzibar, Jamaica, Bermuda, Hong Kong, Singapore, Barbados, Mandalay, Manitoba, Oslo, Osaka, and even Korea. The German Government contributed handsomely, a lady from Lebanon sent a cheque, men of H.M. ships at sea sent their amounts and the French Branch of "Save the Children Fund" forwarded three contributions of one hundred thousand francs each.

Royalty, Presidents, Prime Ministers and Ambassadors made their personal contributions, and these arrived at the Exeter Bank mingled with those spontaneous gestures of small children or with the cheques of Trade Unions, Parish Councils, Friendly Societies and factory staffs.

The first day brought in a total of £25,000. The amount for the second day was £45,800, the next day a further £43,400 and the fourth day, £37,000. The staff at the headquarters of the Fund lost count of days. The figures for the first weeks were:—

First week	...	...	£151,000
After two weeks	...	...	£317,000
After three weeks	...	...	£414,000
After four weeks	...	...	£497,000
After five weeks	...	...	£564,500
After six weeks	...	...	£642,000

In exactly one month, over half a million pounds had been subscribed, and in just under another month the million pound mark was exceeded. The biggest single day's takings was on October 16th, when the total for the day reached the phenomenal figure of £97,079. By October 24th, the Fund had passed the 1¼ million pounds mark.

These figures alone must convey some idea of the enormous amount of work and organisation which went on at the receiving end of the Appeal Fund. Sometimes there were as many as thirty to forty thousand cheques a day, five or six thousand postal orders and on top of these there was the specie. The first parcel of cheques to be sent to the London Clearing House cost £1.93½ in postage. A pointer to the magnificent efforts that were made in dealing with this Fund day by day, was seen by the fact that instead of taking five days to go through the London Clearing House, cheques were taking two days.

This high pressure work went on for eight weeks. It was at the peak of the holiday season. The Bank was busy on its ordinary work and the staff were short-handed through holidays. Everyone, from Mr. Hollis who was responsible, to the newest member of his staff or the most casual volunteer, deserved the highest possible congratulations on a grand job.

The total figure has reached £1,336,425 and before the Appeal Committee began to draw on it, £55 per day interest was accumulating. Up to December 31st, 1952, the interest totalled nearly £6,000.*

---

*The Fund was closed in August, 1956. The interest on the capital totalled £33,605

THE ARMY LENDS A HAND

In times of peace it is seldom possible for the Military to co-operate with local authorities and voluntary organisations on a large scale, but in the immediate and early stages of a disaster the Army can always be relied upon to give help, which will be extended to the completion of the emergency period. It is doubtful if the Forces have ever responded more magnificently than they did over the Lynmouth tragedy.

As has already been shown, Supt. West of Barnstaple contacted local Units about midnight when the floods occurred. It was not until the next morning that the Headquarters of the South Western District at Taunton were informed, and immediately the Chief Engineer, Colonel W. L. Johnson and a General-Staff Officer left for the scene. They found the County Surveyor in charge of engineering work and the Chief Constable of Devon supervising evacuation, and that the local military commanders were, within the limits of their resources, doing all they could to assist.

As requests increased and came from farther afield, however, it became clear that unco-ordinated demands from a variety of civil authorities to a variety of military authorities would be wasteful of effort and lead to confusion, a position moreover further complicated by lack of communications. This matter was therefore settled at the emergency meeting held at the Council Offices, and it was subsequently made quite clear that the Military authorities' duty was to aid the civil power. At no time at Lynmouth did the Army assume any responsibility for the direction of relief or repair work, but at all times Mr. Carnegie was in command.

At this stage too, the extent to which Military authorities were allowed to co-operate was obscure. However, they went on and helped, and then on the Tuesday, Field-Marshal Sir William Slim, Chief of Imperial General Staff, flew to Lynmouth in a helicopter in order to see for himself.

He landed on the Lynton car park and was met by Major General C. L. Firbank, G.O.C., South Western District, and immediately proceeded to inspect the area. His first words were: —"I have come to see if I can be of any assistance, and to see if there is any way the War Office could help General Firbank, who is in charge of the Military assistance being given here." At the conclusion of his inspection Field-Marshal Slim's action was immediate and decisive. He told Mrs. Slater:—
"People here can rely upon it that the Army will do everything they possibly can to help."

He intimated that heavy equipment would be sent, four Bailey bridges would be built and, if necessary, more skilled troops would be sent. They were promises which were fulfilled to the limit. From that moment onwards the Army's initial action became firm policy and they co-operated to the fullest possible extent in every way. Soon after the visit of Field-Marshal Slim, special heavy equipment and more troops were drafted in.

The capacity of both Officers and N.C.O.'s in organising and carrying out work of a technical nature, was a constant reminder of the versatility of the British soldier in the days that followed. It was abundantly proved in the wide variety of tasks undertaken and completed, which included the laying out of the caravan park. Young soldiers laid and jointed drains with man-holes, laid on a water supply with a stand pipe for every caravan, constructed paths, laid tarmac and completed the whole job in thirty hours.

The work in the remote districts was particularly difficult and heavy, involving an average twelve-hour day, sometimes in rain, usually in mud and invariably with somewhat primitive tools. It was never possible to allot the necessary plant, as Lynmouth had priority and in any case, the places where the help was required proved inaccessible to the majority of the heavy equipment. Nevertheless, morale was high, and the highest praise is due to the Regulars, National Service men and "Z" Reservists who, drawn together as individuals or small units from many quarters, worked together harmoniously.

A special task given to nearly one thousand troops at one stage, was the systematic searching for bodies amongst the mass of debris which was piled over a large area of Lynmouth's fore-shore. One young Territorial thus engaged had less than six weeks Army training to his credit, but he willingly undertook the task, remarking as he did so that the Officers were not really making the best use of his technical ability!

Everyone who experienced it, spoke of the morale of the troops as being excellent throughout a very trying time. On their side the Army Authorities could not speak highly enough of the copious quantities of hot tea served at all hours by the Salvation Army and W.V.S. canteens.

The troops worked with a will, partly due to the spontaneous sympathy for the local population and partly an undoubted pride in the job they were doing.

The total work put in by the Military Authorities added up to an impressive total. Hundreds of small services cannot be listed, but in addition one hundred and fourteen farmers were assisted, one hundred and nine different jobs were under-taken for the Police and civilians and a further sixteen for the Ministry of Agriculture.

Those engaged were as follows:—

REGULAR FORMATIONS AND UNITS.

H.Q. SOUTH WESTERN DISTRICT.
43 L.A.A. REGT. R.A.
32 ASSAULT ENGINEER REGT. R.E.
SOUTHERN COMMAND PLANT TROOP R.E.
DEPOT DEVON AND WESSEX BRIGADE.
AMPHIBIOUS WARFARE CENTRE.
22 COMPANY R.A.S.C.
6 DRIVER TRAINING BATTALION R.A.S.C.
15 DRIVER TRAINING BATTALION R.A.S.C.
37 MOBILE BATH COMPANY R.A.O.C.
2 TRAINING BATTALION R.E.M.E.
8 TRAINING BATTALION R.E.M.E.
29 COMMAND WORKSHOPS R.E.M.E.
160 PROVOST COMPANY.

TERRITORIAL ARMY UNITS AND FORMATIONS

264 SCOTTISH BEACH BRIGADE.
121 ARMY ENGINEER REGIMENT (T.A.)
27 ENGINEER GROUP.
102 CORPS ENGINEER REGIMENT (T.A.)
110 FIELD ENGINEER REGIMENT (T.A.)

N.A.A.F.I

THEY ALL WORKED TOGETHER

The work of the various organisations has been mentioned as the occasion arose in the foregoing pages, and the following is a summary of each of these. All who were privileged to see them in action pay tribute to the magnificent team spirit which existed.

THE DEVON CONSTABULARY

The part played by the members of the Police concerned, reflected the highest possible credit on the Force. The little Police Station at Lynton was the nerve centre at the commencement of the tragedy, when at 7.30 on the Friday evening the first call for help was handled by the constable in charge. As the pace increased, so did the tempo at the station.

The normal complement at Lynton and Lynmouth consists of a sergeant in charge and three constables. When the event happened the Sergeant was on leave and one constable off duty. Quite unflurried and unhesitatingly doing the right things, Constables Pavey and Harper carried on. The senior, Constable Earle, returned to duty immediately he heard what was happening. All three of them were concerned in the work of rescue that went on until next day.

Lieut.-Colonel R. R. M. Bacon, Chief Constable of Devon, was early on the scene and in view of the seriousness of the position, decided to stay and take charge. It fell to his lot to make many vital decisions and being able to make them promptly on the spot, valuable time was saved. His foresight and action undoubtedly had a distinct bearing on the subsequent quick recovery. The Walkie-Talkie short wave wireless sets he sent for at the outset proved indispensible, as did his early request to Exeter Airport for aerial reconnaissance. His irrevocable decision to keep the area closed until the influx of people could no longer seriously impair the efficiency of the repair squads, was not popular at the time but has since been appreciated as having been both wise and necessary.

Police headquarters at Middlemoor, near Exeter, were informed of the magnitude of the disaster at 4.30 a.m. on the morning of the 16th August. By noon, Supt. F. W. Doney in charge of traffic and operations had achieved wonders. The walkie-talkie outfits had been collected from Bristol and delivered at Lynton and transport had been sent from all over Devon for reinforcement. A land rover equipped with wireless was operating at Lynmouth and patrol cars and motor-cycle despatch riders were assisting in the work. In addition, an Operations Room at Headquarters was in being, handling hundreds of incoming calls.

Inspector Burgess and Motor Patrol Sergeant Edwards rose to the occasion too, in finding a hazardous way through for the R.A.F. and amphibious teams in the early hours of Saturday morning.

In the days that followed, the Force was reinforced from all corners of Devon until there was a total of forty-seven personnel engaged.

Supt. Doney took charge of the area when Lieut.-Col. Bacon returned to Headquarters.

The duties that fell to the Police were very wide and included traffic control, Information Bureau and Missing Persons Register, receiving and recording of all property, evacuation of the people, the search for and identification of bodies—to name a few. There were inquests to be arranged, important people to be received and conducted and above all, restoration of order. Their calmness and confidence were at once a tonic and an example to all with whom they came into contact. On all sides afterwards one heard of their kindness and courtesy to those who had suffered tragic loss.

Constable Harper, then only sixteen months in the service lived up to its highest traditions in his work on the first night. He did $25\frac{1}{2}$ hours continuous duty, and some days later went down a seven hundred foot cliff on the end of a rope, searching for bodies. His attitude on being congratulated was, "anyone would have done the same under the same set of circumstances".

The *esprit de corps* shown by Sergeant Burnard and Constables Pavey, Harper and Earle, upon whom the major portion of the purely local work naturally fell, was very fine indeed. The latter was in charge of the mortuary services during the whole period.

At Barnstaple, the Divisional Office became a nerve centre. Supt. A. E. West and his staff were the police contact with the outside world, and as has already been described, handled thousands of calls and collated and passed on the vital information which did so much to relieve anxiety.

Throughout the whole emergency period, the greatest assistance was given and received by the Somerset County Police, which was represented in the Lynmouth area by sixteen of the Force. An equal number of Royal Military Police proved invaluable.

Later, the Chief Constable's commendation for outstanding work, which is given only in exceptional cases, was presented to Superintendent A. E. West, Superintendent L. T. Burgess and Sergeant A. V. Burnard.

Personnel of the Devon Constabulary engaged included:
LIEUT.-COLONEL R. R. M. BACON.
Superintendents: F. W. DONEY. A. E. WEST.
Inspectors: L. T. BURGESS. H. F. WHEELER.
Sergeants: H. PEARDON, W. BOND, A. WALTERS, A. V.
BURNARD, J. BARNES, A. FOGWILL, A. HORWOOD, I.
MORGAN, J. MOORE and M/P SGT. E. RICHARDS; also
thirty-four Constables.

*   *   *

THE DEVON COUNTY FIRE SERVICE

It has already been told how the services of the Fire Brigade
were called upon at the very outset of the disaster, and the action
and initiative shown by the two teams based on Lynton were
highly praiseworthy, as was their rescue work in the early hours
of the morning. When the flooding became general, however, a
call for volunteers was sent out from Headquarters over the whole
of the country and the response from each of the fifty-one
stations was immediate.

Except for a nucleus of full-time personnel, the majority are
retained men who follow their normal day to day employment,
but make themselves available to respond at any time for fire
service duty. Strictly speaking, none of the duties these men
carried out at Lynmouth were fire service duties—rather they
were duties which have perhaps become accepted as part of their
role since the war.

Be that as it may. The work they did was generally speaking
most unpleasant and unspectacular. Where cellars contained
only water they were pumped dry, cleansed and disinfected, but
so many of them were absolutely jammed with silt, mud and in
some cases heavy boulders, trees and debris. The removal of
these tons of material from the basements, cellars and other parts

of flooded buildings had to be most carefully and systematically carried out, in order that everything salvable was recovered. It often necessitated the sifting of mud through bare hands. In this way too, at least one body was discovered lying under feet of silt. No other branch of any Service took part in this work of clearing and cleansing.

In addition owners were generally assisted in salvaging property, buildings were weatherproofed and in a hundred and one different ways help was given cheerfully and willingly to all who needed it. In those first days, faced with what seemed to be insurmountable difficulties, the phrase for both residents and organisations became "*Send for the Fire Brigade*".

Under the supervision of food inspectors they removed and destroyed tons of contaminated foodstuffs. They carried goods for the W.V.S. and the Salvation Army, and water for the population. They shored up buildings and boarded up windows. All these duties were carried out by men who might have been carrying on with their own job undisturbed, miles away.

Due to the difficulty of feeding and billeting, not more than fifty men were based on Lynmouth at one time but a rota system was worked by volunteers drawn from stations all over Devon. Of the total of more than four hundred who volunteered for service, two hundred and ten officers and men carried on continuous duty for twenty days.

Apart altogether from their general assistance in the searching for bodies, there was no one else available to undertake the work of burial parties, and here again the Fire Service stepped in, acting as bearers and performing many other tasks in connection with the funerals that took place.

The training and discipline of the Fire Service was in evidence throughout the whole operation, and clearly demonstrates the versatility of service which has become the tradition of the organisation.

Personnel engaged:—

    Chief Fire Officer: W. H. BARKER, O.B.E.
    Station Officers: F. WATLING (HQ), W. POTTER
    (Paignton).
    208 Other Ranks.

*   *   *

THE PART PLAYED BY TRANSPORT

On the night of the flood the last bus of the Southern National public transport left Lynton at 8.30, coinciding with the bus leaving Barnstaple at the same time. The Lynton bus got through, but the incoming vehicle which was routed via Parracombe had a difficult journey. It must have left the village just before the bridge gave way, and then from Dean Steep ran into difficulties. No progress at all was possible beyond Barbrook. There were eight passengers, who with the driver and conductor were marooned owing to the torrential downpour. When it eased about 2 a.m., they decided to abandon the vehicle—one of many then stranded—and attempt to get to Lynton through the woods. It was a difficult journey in the darkness, but was successfully accomplished.

Meanwhile Mr. H. J. Sutton, the inspector in charge of the Lynton depot, having checked that the bus had left Barnstaple, realised that it could never get through and so took a vehicle to the top of Lynbridge Cross as near to Barbrook as possible, where he was able to assess the situation and assist in urgent local relief operations.

Directly it began to get light next morning, it was seen that some transport to assist those fleeing from the stricken village below was a necessity. The first on the scene in this respect was Mr. Bob Jones, who took his lorry down Lynmouth Hill at about 4.30 a.m. He thus commenced an indispensable shuttle service. The bus inspector saw that one vehicle would be quite inadequate and obtaining Police permission hurried back to the depot and himself drove a 29-seater vehicle down to the ever increasing crowd of weary people, gathering at the foot of the hill as the waters receded, enabling some to leave places where they had been isolated all night. As more and more people were rescued from buildings surrounded by water, they too, were directed to the foot of the hill. It is an amazing tribute to the patience of all concerned, that after the first load of passengers had gone, those who waited silently formed the normal queue, just as though it was "business as usual" at an ordinary bus stop.

The bus and the lorry did countless journeys and it was estimated that up to midday on Saturday, over six hundred people with such belongings as they had rescued, were carried up the hill to the rest centres. It was a fine work, which it is doubtful has ever been fully appreciated. Mr. Carnegie later instituted a similar system on Monday morning with two vans which continued the shuttle service for a month, until it was no longer required.

Early on Saturday morning the first bus from Barnstaple with a number of relief drivers, made a way through into Lynton. The water had receded from the road at Barbrook sufficiently to allow the bus to pass, although a large portion of the road had slipped into the gorge. The receding waters had left a mass of debris, stranded motor-cars and boulders on the road. The drivers tugged and strained at boulders and trees and even man-handled cars to clear a way and then, recovering the bus which had been stranded the previous night, eventually made their way through.

In the season, Saturday is always a change-over day. Then in August some hundreds of visitors left Lynton with a like number coming in. On this tragic occasion it was twice as hectic as usual, and some pathetic and heart-breaking scenes were witnessed. Soon after 8 a.m. visitors, who the day before were preparing to return to their homes all over the country refreshed after a holiday, began to arrive at the Bus Company's office. Many had only the clothes they stood up in; some had small parcels—all that remained of their baggage; others were perturbed about the fate of friends, and many had lost their tickets. Some were dejected, weary and dazed after the nightmare experience of the previous twelve hours; others displayed a spirit of fortitude that was amazing.

The employees of the Bus Company responded nobly to the occasion, and nowhere was the British spirit better exemplified. They gave comfort, cheerful assistance and in a great many cases lent money to those who were starting back from a tragic holiday, penniless.

That day it was one-way traffic, a general exodus, and more than six hundred visitors were carried from the town to Barnstaple, where they made connection with the railway that took them to their destinations.

Like those in every trade and profession, the busmen did not escape unscathed and six of their number suffered in the upheaval. Without question—and incidentally without overtime —their colleagues filled their places and carried on until they could be replaced.

Public transport and those connected with it played a very commendable and important part in the aftermath of the floods.

*   *   *

BRITISH RED CROSS

The Devonshire Branch of the British Red Cross Society set their organisation in motion immediately they heard of the disaster, and it was fortunate that both Countess Fortescue (County President) and Countess Eldon (Vice President) were easily accessible.

Lady Fortescue made instant arrangements for a supply of mattresses, blankets and pillows to be placed at the disposal of those at the Rest Centres, and Lady Eldon quickly arrived on the scene, which she rarely left for the next six weeks. Her organising ability and enthusiasm were invaluable and her efforts to form, equip and run the Holman Caravan Park were crowned with success.

A Red Cross medical loan and hardware store was set up in the Town Hall, where in the early stages a First Aid service with two nurses in attendance was also in great demand. The London headquarters were telephoned for stores, which were sent down by convoy immediately.

Assistance and supplies were also given to Rest Centres, and personnel were sent to help at the First Aid post that had been set up by the St. John Ambulance Association at the foot of Lynmouth Hill. Subsequently an emergency centre was set up in Lynton. Constant supervision at Rest Centres which were in operation over the whole Exmoor area, was maintained by the members of the Lynmouth Headquarters. Altogether six members were on duty daily and two every night on a rota system, for well over a month personnel came from all over the country.

The depot at the Town Hall proved indispensable, for approximately seven thousand articles were issued. The Caravan Park already mentioned caused many to bless the British Red Cross Society.

Personnel engaged were under the direction of Lady Fortescue (President), Lady Eldon (Vice President) and Lieut.-General Sir Treffry Thompson (County Director).

*   *   *

ST. JOHN AMBULANCE BRIGADE

It has already been told how the local division of the St. John Ambulance Brigade were involved from the commencement of the disaster, the local Superintendent receiving a call at 7.45 on Friday evening.

When the extent of the flood damage was appreciated outside, the senior County Officials working under the North Devon Area Commissioner immediately alerted the County organisation and an ambulance was sent from the County depot in addition to the Barnstaple vehicle already on the spot. All vehicles in the North Devon area were ready to respond to a call had they been needed. In addition to normal work, ambulances were placed at the disposal of the Police as required, for the removal of bodies.

The work of every individual member of the local division was deserving of the highest congratulation, and there is no doubt that the First Aid post set up at the foot of Lynmouth Hill rendered fine service.

As the work progressed several major accidents occurred and many serious cases dealt with. When an Army lorry overturned, there were six serious cases consisting of fractured and broken arms and legs and bad lacerations. When an Army tractor met with an accident, one man suffered a badly crushed foot and after initial treatment by the St. John Ambulance Brigade, had to be rushed to the hospital at Barnstaple.

Those engaged did not stop at ambulance duties. They assisted in the work of rescue, evacuation and the supply and transport of stores, as well as numerous other good works which required to be done and were executed efficiently and willingly without question.

Several members of the local Brigade suffered personal loss but carried on notwithstanding with their ambulance duties. One man lost his home entirely and those of two others were badly damaged. Private E. Smith, who a few weeks before had received a Certificate of Merit for his part in a car accident on Countisbury Hill, lost his life in the disaster.

Personnel engaged included:—Dr. M. P. Nightingale, Divisional Surgeon of Lynton and Lynmouth Division; Area

Superintendent R. G. Rogers; Area Officer R. J. Braddon; Area Superintendent Miss Valentine; Superintendents and Members of Ambulance Divisions of Lynton and Lynmouth, Barnstaple, Ilfracombe, Braunton, Combe Martin, Bideford and South Molton; and Nursing Divisions of Barnstaple, Bideford and Braunton.

*   *   *

Mention must also be made here of the great assistance and co-operation shewn by Lt.-Col. C. H. Condon, Devon County Ambulance Officer, who was responsible for the fullest possible co-ordination of the Ambulance Services.

*   *   *

WOMEN'S VOLUNTARY SERVICE

The familiar dark green uniforms of the W.V.S. were first observed on the scene early on Saturday, when the advance guard arrived with thermostatic urns of tea, and thereafter teams of twelve members drawn from various centres throughout the county worked night and day on a rota system. They controlled the Rest Centres, set up a clothing store, supplied and ran a mobile canteen consisting of three vehicles which arrived from Bristol, and in short were the fount and inspiration of the grand welfare work that was carried on.

If the residents of Lynmouth were grateful for the help which descended on them from all over the world, the W.V.S. was positively embarrassed. At the clothing depot an enormous volume of goods was handled, until the full effect of the nation-wide appeal was felt and it became too large to be handled at Lynton. As recounted elsewhere, a depot was set up at Newton Abbot.

Emergency feeding teams took over the Rest Centre at Jubilee Hall, and produced approximately two hundred and twenty breakfasts and three hundred midday meals daily for the homeless folk, firemen and other workers. The total number of main meals supplied over the whole period was 18,000. In addition, a regular supply of sandwiches and urns of tea were sent out daily to the scene of operations.

In the fitting-out of those people who had lost their all, a magnificent work was done. Nearly 8,000 articles of clothing were issued to well over a thousand people.

In conjunction with the Ministry of Food, the members of the W.V.S. distributed the five tons of bananas and sugar which had been sent from Jamaica.

The kindly and understanding way in which the ladies assisted those who applied to them for help, was greatly appreciated by all and the work went on until once again Lynmouth was opened to the outside world.

The work was set in motion by Miss E. M. Powell, Devon County Organiser W.V.S., who carried on until her presence was necessary at the depot at Newton Abbot. She was then relieved by her deputy, Miss M. C. A. Paynter. The Rest Centre and feeding arrangements were under the supervision of Mrs. E. A. Stanley, South West Regional Officer of the W.V.S. for emergency feeding. For weeks this lady ate, slept and worked on the job. Teams of W.V.S. volunteers from all Centres in the county worked in relays until the need was past.

*   *   *

SALVATION ARMY

The Salvation Army, true to tradition, answered the call for help. Mobile canteens were despatched with all speed and Salvation Army officers moved in to help with the work of feeding and the rehabilitation of the people.

The men and women worked unceasingly and efficiently. Their mobile canteen was in the front line of operations, and Army "lassies" volunteered from London, Plymouth, Bath, Bideford and other centres.

Many an official, service man and civilian workman were maintained and cheered by the cup of tea and a bun, provided by the Salvation Army workers and the appreciative remarks were in themselves a glowing testimony to the grand work of the Salvation Army.

Religious services were held in open spaces in the town in the evenings, and were well attended by soldiers and civilians.

* * *

R. S. P. C. A.

In times of distress to human beings, the saving of lives and alleviation of suffering to animals could perhaps be forgotten, but at Lynmouth the R.S.P.C.A. Inspectors and officials of the Sick Animals Dispensary were early on the scene and worked unceasingly in their efforts to find and remove to a place of safety, animals and pets belonging to the homeless. John Ambrose of Barnstaple and John Pickett of Exeter, both inspectors of the R.S.P.C.A., risked their lives continually in searching wrecked homes and insecure buildings.

It was obvious that not only human beings forget their differences in time of trouble, for in one corner covered by debris, a tortoise and a rabbit were found snuggling together under a bed. Three Pekinese dogs were found playing together in a lonely spot elsewhere. Two goats, thirty cats, ten dogs and a number of fowls, ferrets, pigeons and even goldfish, were recovered and put into places of safety until their owners could think of them and take steps to reclaim them.

Often the discovery of an animal in distress and its rescue were two very different things. The recovery of a fowl alone meant an arduous journey through floods, and from a precarious position on a cliff, some forty fowl were recovered in a pitiable condition. Thirty-eight of them subsequently revived.

The London Headquarters of the organisation offered help, and immediately responded when asked for an animal ambulance. The driver of the vehicle not only drove through the night to get to Lynmouth, but on arrival worked all day as well.

When the work of clearing and blasting operations commenced, those animals still at large became terrified and greatly complicated the work of rescue. In all, one hundred and two animals and pets were recovered from the shambles in Lynmouth and Challacombe areas by the officials of the R.S.P.C.A.

Great bravery was shown by a twelve-year-old-girl, Jennifer Pearce, who on the night of the flood braved the waters and risked her life to rescue her pony.

At a ceremony held at Lynton Town Hall some months afterwards, several awards were made by Countess Fortescue on behalf of the R.S.P.C.A. Jennifer Pearce received the R.S.P.C.A. Silver Medal and other awards were as follows:—

Mrs. J. Ambrose, Queen Victoria Silver Medal;

Inspector J. Ambrose, Queen Victoria Silver Medal;

Inspector J. Pickett, Queen Victoria Silver Medal;

Miss M. Mackay (Hon. Secretary to the North Devon Branch), Queen Victoria Medal.

*   *   *

POST OFFICE TELEPHONES

The telephone system at Lynton and Lynmouth was centred on a small (unattended) robot exchange perched high above Lynmouth and beyond the reach of the floods.

When the trouble started by a number of lines in Lynmouth going dead, the robot signalled Barnstaple exchange by setting off an alarm bell. This led to enquiries, and Post Office engineers who set off to rectify matters found a whole lot of trouble. More and more lines went dead and then, to make the situation worse, the main cable link with Barnstaple went out of action. This severed all connection not only with the twin villages but also Brendon and Parracombe, all of which became entirely cut off from the outside world.

In Lynmouth itself, flood water swept away earthenware duct pipes, the cables contained in them, concrete underground chambers, poles and wires and even two public telephone kiosks were dislodged and never seen again.

Hampered by the chaotic conditions and awful weather, engineers worked frantically all night and at last succeeded in restoring communication to a limited extent by 2 p.m. on the Saturday afternoon. The full restoration was made nine hours later. Altogether thirty-four junction circuits affecting three hundred and twenty-five subscribers had been put out of action.

Meanwhile, as has been described elsewhere, enormous demands were being made on the Barnstaple Exchange, and Post Office engineers installed emergency lines and telephone equipment for the Police and scores of organisations who were assisting. There were lines provided for the B.B.C., and the extra heavy traffic to Barnstaple and the Press had to be provided for, not only for their normal stories but also for the transmission of pictures to their London offices.

As soon as possible work was started on a normal reconnection and many clever improvisations were made as temporary expedients. In order to put Brendon back on the telephone, a rope was thrown across the river and a cable pulled over, where it remained looped until its temporary purpose had been served.

No department had a greater strain thrown upon it by the emergency, and none rose to the occasion more efficiently.

*   *   *

ELECTRICITY SERVICE

In an earlier chapter reference is made to the fact that Lynton and Lynmouth were lit by electricity as early as 1890, and throughout all those years it had operated successfully until the night of the floods. When the lights finally went out that night, it was the end for all time of the generation of electricity at 100 cycle frequency for public supply in the whole of Great Britain. Among the first in the whole country to operate, Lynmouth's was the last of the old style to capitulate.

When the floods receded on the morning of August 16th, the South Western Electricity Board engineers were ready to start work, and one hundred and twenty men tackled the enormous problem of restoring supplies, which were to come from the National Grid. In the afternoon two days later partial though rationed supplies were available, and on August 21st a full supply was connected to the whole town, including Lynbridge and Barbrook. This was a great achievement considering that no section of workmen ever had a clear field, but were hampered by groups of a score of other organisations working in the same area.

When the County Surveyor asked for assistance in maintaining a round-the-clock working, the North Devon District Manager, Mr. R. Robinson, fitted and connected up a large battery of floodlamps, which were of inestimable value to those working in the hours of darkness.

THE FUTURE IS ASSURED

The speed at which the work proceeded was beyond the wildest hopes of everybody. There was still some concern however, about the spring tides due on September 2nd and 3rd. The height of water in these tides was formerly controlled by the harbour bar, but, of course, this had disappeared in the flood. Troops were therefore put to work erecting a temporary embankment above the thousands of tons of boulders and rubble which had been pushed to the side of the river channel, and thousands of sandbags made a workmanlike "wall". It was an anxious few days, and all night long searchlights were trained on the water, so that any rise would be immediately detected. Although the tides ran fairly high, no breach was made. This concern was repeated following heavy thunderstorms which broke over the valley on September 6th. Again an anxious vigil was kept, but all was well.

A further cause for concern was the 12,000 tons of boulders and debris, which were still poised threateningly in the gorge above Lynmouth. It was felt that if a rainfall as heavy as four inches was to occur, all this material would probably get on the move again and there would be a repetition of the August disaster.

Although continual requests had been made to the Police for the re-opening of the roads in Lynton, it was considered neither sensible nor practicable to do so until September 2nd. The Police had set the time of re-opening for midday, but long before that time a variety of people jostled one another expectantly

at the barriers erected outside Lynton. Cars, coaches and lorries
—some on business, some simply sight-seeing—had arrived,
but the Police were adamant—12 noon and not before.

At last the emergency phase was completed, and the Army
began to move out, completing their evacuation on September
11th, 1952.

The day of the full re-opening of Lynmouth drew near.
The fact that there had been so little time lag reflects the greatest credit on all concerned. Lynmouth had been transformed
from the chaos of a month before. True, its scars were there for
all to see—shored up buildings, boarded windows, gaps where
buildings had simply disappeared. For all that, it was still
Lynmouth. On the walls of buildings was the mark "FL" pain-
ted in red, and these flood level marks are as honourable as the
scars resulting from that one terrible night.

The shops had been re-stocked. There was an air of expec-
tancy, and Lynmouth people were breathing freely again. This
was the beginning of a new future, which they had thought impossible a few weeks back. The first vehicle to bring supplies
a day before, was a brewer's lorry and County Council workmen
raised their HATS and gave it an ovation.

It was a good omen that Saturday, September 13th, 1952,
was a bright sunny day, and at noon a large gathering assembled
round a flag staff that had been erected at the car park. And so,
as the Union Jack was broken out, Mrs. D. Slater, the Chairman
of the Urban District Council, who had done such magnificent
work throughout the whole period, officially re-opened the village.
It was exactly four weeks after the calamity.

The same afternoon the first public service vehicle from
Minehead to make contact with Lynmouth, drove over the bridge
from Countisbury Hill and it received a noisy welcome. Shops

displayed "Business as Usual" notices. Lynmouth was again in its stride welcoming visitors.

Even Tim, the little dog belonging to Tom Floyd, seemed proud of his medal. When the newspapers carried the story of his escape, a wellwisher from London had sent a pound note so that Tim could have a new collar and a medallion with the inscription:—"To Tim who survived the Floods, August 15th. 1952."

For a hundred years it has been the tradition that on Boxing Day the Exmoor Hunt meet at the Lyndale Hotel, and it was a pleasing thought that, although the meeting place could not be the same hotel as it was out of commission, they still met on December 26th, 1952, but at the Rising Sun Hotel.

In November the first post-flood wedding took place at Lynmouth Church. The village was coming back into its own. Much may have altered but the spirit of the people was the same. It is, therefore, needless to ask—"What of the future?" Perhaps the old Lynmouth can never be entirely recaptured, but what can be in this changing world?

Lynmouth will undoubtedly rise again to its pre-eminence as a beauty spot of untold loveliness. In addition, as time goes on, the busy tourist trade will be restored and even extended. Lynmouth made millions of new friends in the days that followed the tremendous publicity the disaster received, and undoubtedly a high proportion of those new friends will visit Lynton and Lynmouth, and whoever visits these beautiful twin villages just once?

The Council and the experts are united in their desire to make the new Lynmouth as near the old as possible. May it be so, and worthy in every way of the courage and fortitude of its people on that unforgettable night.

POSTSCRIPT

LYNTON and LYNMOUTH have recovered from that tragic night in 1952, the results of which, considering the size of the villages, were terrible. Thirty-four people were killed or missing; 93 houses and buildings destroyed or subsequently demolished; 28 bridges destroyed or badly damaged and 132 vehicles were destroyed.

The work which has been carried out to ensure no possible recurrence of the tragedy, has been tried and tested in extreme tidal conditions and found not only safe but safe with a tremendous margin. The glorious surroundings of the twin villages were never dimmed, and in recent years holiday-makers from all over the country and tourists from all over the world, have been coming again to this lovely part of Devon.

*   *   *

Lynmouth was officially re-opened on September 13th, 1952, and before and since that date no less than 114,000 tons of debris has been removed from river channels, roads and harbours.

The new Harbour Arm and the Tower were rebuilt during 1954.

The Lyndale and Lynmouth Street bridges were opened in June 1954.

Barbrook's new bridge to repace the temporary Bailey bridge built by the Royal Engineers, was opened in September, 1956.

The expenditure of emergency works immediately after the flood totalled £75,000. Permanent reconstruction, the bulk of the finance which was supplied by the Government and a considerable amount by the Devon County Council, amounted in all to £650,000.

The Flood Memorial Building was completed early in 1958.

In August, 1956, the Relief Fund was wound up and in the four years it had been in existence had reached £1,336,425, all of which was distributed to the 1,710 people who suffered in the disaster.

The total cost of administration, amounting to some £11,145 and certain other expenses, were met from the interest on capital, estimated at £36,605. The remaining £20,000 of this figure has been handed over to Trustees.

Provision for the dependants of those who lost their lives is made by a £34,394 Trust Fund.

*   *   *

Mr. R. B. Carnegie, County Surveyor, whose health suffered considerably as a result of his exertions during the emergency, died suddenly on September 1st, 1961. In May, 1962, a plaque on the bridge at the foot of Countisbury Hill was unveiled. It reads:

TO COMMEMORATE

ROBERT BLACK CARNEGIE, C.B.E.

COUNTY SURVEYOR OF DEVON

WHO DIRECTED THE RELIEF

AND SUBSEQUENT RE-BUILDING

OF LYNMOUTH AFTER THE

FLOOD DISASTER OF 1952

Other books by Eric Delderfield include:

NORTH DEVON STORY

About Lynton and Lynmouth and its old railway, the Lift, Coaching Days, Barnstaple Fair etc.

EXMOOR WANDERINGS

Stories of the Shepherds, the Exmoor Mining Days, the Red Deer, Dunster and Minehead.

BRIEF GUIDE TO EXMOOR

An extremely popular little handbook for all who are on a brief visit and wish to know essential details about the countryside.

WEST COUNTRY HISTORIC HOUSES AND THEIR FAMILIES

3 Vols. profusely illustrated.

BRITISH INN SIGNS AND THEIR STORIES

With over 200 illustrations.

ERIC DELDERFIELD'S BOOK OF TRUE ANIMAL STORIES

Illustrated. 2 Vols.
3 Vols. now in Pan paperbacks.

KINGS AND QUEENS OF ENGLAND

Gives in a brief form the principle dates, happenings and accomplishments of the reigns of all the monarchs. Illustrated.

Obtainable from all Booksellers or E.R.D. Publications Ltd., 53 Strand Exmouth, Devon.